*PARADISE LOST*

# LIVES OF GREAT RELIGIOUS BOOKS

# Paradise Lost

## A BIOGRAPHY

ALAN JACOBS

PRINCETON UNIVERSITY PRESS

PRINCETON & OXFORD

Published by Princeton University Press
41 William Street, Princeton, New Jersey 08540
99 Banbury Road, Oxford OX2 6JX

press.princeton.edu

GPSR Authorized Representative: Easy Access System Europe - Mustamäe tee 50, 10621 Tallinn, Estonia, gpsr.requests@easproject.com

Library of Congress Cataloging-in-Publication Data
Names: Jacobs, Alan, 1958– author.
Title: Paradise Lost : a biography / Alan Jacobs.
Description: Princeton : Princeton University Press, 2025. |
    Series: Lives of great religious books | Includes bibliographical
    references and index.
Identifiers: LCCN 2024036083 (print) | LCCN 2024036084 (ebook) |
    ISBN 9780691238579 (hardback) | ISBN 9780691238586 (ebook)
    Subjects: LCSH: Milton, John, 1608–1674. Paradise lost. | Milton,
    John, 1608–1674—Influence. | Milton, John, 1608–1674—
    Appreciation. | BISAC: LITERARY CRITICISM / Poetry |
    RELIGION / Religion, Politics & State | LCGFT: Literary criticism.
Classification: LCC PR3562 .J17 2025 (print) | LCC PR3562 (ebook) |
    DDC 821/.4—dc23/eng/20240828
LC record available at https://lccn.loc.gov/2024036083
LC ebook record available at https://lccn.loc.gov/2024036084

British Library Cataloging-in-Publication Data is available

Editorial: Fred Appel and James Collier
Production Editorial: Sara Lerner
Jacket Design: Wanda España
Production: Erin Suydam
Publicity: Alyssa Sanford and Charlotte Coyne
Copyeditor: Anne Cherry

Jacket Credit: Watercolor illustration to *Paradise Lost* by William Blake, the Butts set, 1808

This book has been composed in Arno

Printed in the United States of America

10  9  8  7  6  5  4  3  2  1

For Laity Lodge, place and people

.

Milton's poem is admirable in this respect, since it is impossible for any of its readers, whatever nation, country, or people he may belong to, not to be related to the persons who are the principal actors in it; but what is still infinitely more to its advantage, the principal actors in this poem are not only our progenitors, but our representatives. We have an actual interest in everything they do, and no less than our utmost happiness is concerned and lies at stake in all their behavior.

—JOSEPH ADDISON

Has any great poem ever let in so little light upon one's own joys and sorrows? I get no help in judging life; I scarcely feel that Milton lived or knew men and women.

—VIRGINIA WOOLF

The poem is not good in spite of but especially because of its moral confusions, which ought to be clear in your mind when you are feeling its power. I think it horrible and wonderful; I regard it as like Aztec or Benin sculpture, or to come nearer home the novels of Kafka, and am rather suspicious of any critic who claims not to feel anything so obvious.

—WILLIAM EMPSON

# CONTENTS

# PREFACE

THE INCLUSION of *Paradise Lost* in a series called Lives of the Great Religious Books should immediately prompt the reader to ask whether *Paradise Lost*—which is an epic poem, not a sacred text or a devotional treatise or guide—is a religious book at all. But of course this cannot be answered without asking what "religious" means, and, I suppose, what "religion" is. These are all questions that at the outset of my task I must face, or else skillfully evade.

Many years ago I heard it said—I wish I could remember by whom—that the only thing the world's religions have in common is that they all use candles. Thus Sir James Frazer, in beginning his great *The Golden Bough*, wrote that "There is probably no subject in the world about which opinions differ so much as the nature of religion, and to frame a definition of it which would satisfy every one must obviously be impossible. All that a writer can do is, first, to say clearly what he means by religion, and afterwards to employ the word consistently in that sense throughout his work."[1] I hope not even to

---

1. James Frazer, *The Golden Bough: A Study in Magic and Religion*, abridged edition (London: Penguin, 1996 [1922]), p. 60. This is from the famous Chapter IV, "Magic and Religion."

do that much, but rather to point out that there are, very broadly speaking, two approaches to the definition of religion, and only according to one of them can *Paradise Lost* be considered a religious book.

According to a *functional* definition of religion—which, should I ever be forced to choose, is the one I would probably opt for[2]—a religion is essentially a set of social practices; according to a *dogmatic* definition a religion is a essentially a set of shared beliefs. Now, to be sure, no useful approach to religion can do without either practices or beliefs; but one can think of religion as a set of practices with attached beliefs or a set of beliefs with attached practices. It is a matter of emphasis. And *Paradise Lost* is a story so distant from any of the practices of any known religion that I cannot see any way to qualify it as a religious book under that approach. For all religious practices look to repair or deepen a relationship with a god or gods, or some divine being or principle, and what need for any of those endeavors have people who dwell in the unbroken, undimmed, and constant presence of their Creator? (That is a definitive statement that may in time require some nuancing; but for now let it stand.)

2. Emile Durkheim's definition is a useful one: "*A religion is a unified system of beliefs and practices relative to sacred things, that is to say, things set apart and surrounded by prohibitions—beliefs and practices that unite its adherents in single moral community called a church*": Emile Durkheim, *The Elementary Forms of the Religious Life*, trans. Carol Cosman (Oxford: Oxford University Press, 2001 [1912]), p. 46; italics in original. Durkheim is using the term *church* in a very broad sense, though one may doubt whether it can possibly be broad enough to cover all relevant cases. This definition contains both functional and dogmatic elements, but as Durkheim unfolds his conceptual frame the functional strongly dominates.

Thus C. S. Lewis, who strongly believed that *Paradise Lost* is a work firmly emplaced in the Christian tradition that he himself affirmed, nevertheless also said,

> I think it is quite true that in some very important senses it is not a religious poem. If a Christian reader has found his devotion quickened by reading the medieval hymns or Dante or [George] Herbert or [Thomas] Traherne, or even by [Coventry] Patmore or [William] Cowper, and then turns to *Paradise Lost,* he will be disappointed. How cold, how heavy and external it will all seem! How many blankets seem to be interposed between us and our object!

So *Paradise Lost* offers no help for those who wish to "quicken," or deepen, or even inform, the devotional practices of the religious life. If one comes to it for such help, one cannot but be left cold. That noted, Lewis continues, "I am not sure that *Paradise Lost* was intended to be a religious poem in the sense suggested, and I am sure it need not be." What, then, does the poem hope to do?

> It is a poem depicting the objective pattern of things, the attempted destruction of that pattern by rebellious self-love, and the triumphant absorption of that rebellion into a yet more complex pattern. The cosmic story—the ultimate plot in which all other stories are episodes—is set before us. We are invited, for the time being, to look at it from outside. And that is not, in itself, a religious exercise.[3]

3. C. S. Lewis, *A Preface to "Paradise Lost"* (London: Oxford University Press, 1942), p. 132.

No—not "a religious exercise," if religion is primarily charac-
terized by certain *practices*. But if religion is primarily a matter
of *beliefs*, is seen as intrinsically and centrally dogmatic or
theological? Then in that case *Paradise Lost* is an essentially
religious poem, for in it Milton is passionately concerned to
identify certain central beliefs of the Christian faith, to portray
them dramatically, and to expose their significance for those
of us who live in the aftermath of the Eden story. (That is, for
all of *us*.) That Milton's poem is indeed religious *in this sense*
can be discerned from the intensity of responses it has received over the centuries. Dante is as theological a poet as
Milton, but Dante's theology is typically situated within a context of recognizable human struggle; which is why Erich Auerbach calls him the "poet of the secular world" and also why
he rarely inspires hatred.[4] Milton's writing about religion "from
outside"—seemingly from above, from some Olympian
height—has helped make him one of the most despised writers
in history, and *Paradise Lost* one of the most despised poems,
though also one of the most admired. I hope the following
pages will show that throughout Milton's poem there is a high-
tension ambivalence about being "a religious book" that makes
it hard to ignore and, once encountered, impossible to forget.

*Paradise Lost* is above all an epic poem, and that means, as
Milton and his predecessors in the genre would have agreed,
it is a *heroic* poem, a poem narrating heroic action. The problem with those predecessors of his, Milton thought, was that
they did not understand what is truly epic and truly heroic—

4. Erich Auerbach, *Dante: Poet of the Secular World* (New York: New York Review Classics, 2007).

or, for that matter, truly tragic. At the outset of Book IX, which describes the Fall of Adam and Eve from their state of innocence, Milton declares "I now must change / Those notes to tragic"—the notes of his great and solemn poetic music. It is, he says, a "sad task," but it is one worth pursuing, because the "argument" he must make—that is, the story he must tell, along with the vital inferences to be drawn from the course it follows—is

> Not less but more heroic than the wrath
> Of stern Achilles on his foe pursued
> Thrice fugitive about Troy wall; or rage
> Of Turnus for Lavinia disespoused,
> Or Neptune's ire or Juno's, that so long
> Perplexed the Greek and Cytherea's son . . . (IX.14–19)

Thus the *Iliad*, the *Aeneid*, and the *Odyssey*, in that order, are said by Milton to have described matters of far less import than the ones he describes. Even the tale of Rome's founding is of merely local and temporary interest in comparison to the event that "Brought death into the world, and all our woe" (I.3). Whatever their gifts as poets, Homer and Virgil were hamstrung by *religious* inadequacies: they lacked a true understanding of the world, of the origin and nature of humanity, of the identity of the true God. Milton, in writing this poem, is doubly correcting his predecessors' errors: by stating the case for the true religion, he is also stating the case for a redefinition of epic and heroic poetry. He redefines greatness in the writing of verse. It is the combination of this bold revisionary strategy with Milton's staggering power as a poet that makes his poem's later career so fascinating and so worthy of telling. In writing

*Paradise Lost* Milton initiated battle on two fronts, the religious and the poetic, and those battles have continued apace in the three and a half centuries since his death. People have continued to care about poetry, and about religion, and Milton's poem has been a lighning-rod, drawing to itself the electrical energies of those passions. That's why this book was worth writing—and why, I meekly suggest, it's worth reading.

———

I am not a Miltonist, though I have sometimes longed to be one. In graduate school, many years ago, I had every intention of specializing in British literature of the seventeenth century—with Milton looming inevitably large in my picture of the era—until, in my very last course, under the tutelage of the brilliant (but now, alas, departed) Daniel Albright, I encountered the poetry and prose of W. H. Auden and consequently altered my professional trajectory radically and permanently. But I never forgot Milton, nor have I neglected him, in part because I have taught *Paradise Lost* almost every year for the past thirty-five years. I don't suppose there's any other book I have read so many times, and certainly none that has more richly rewarded my best attention. Moreover, there's no poem I'd rather teach: for my students it's often inscrutable and off-putting, and they tend to dislike Milton personally, and because I have many of the same responses myself, all of us in the classroom enter the contest together. I may sometimes *feel* as they feel about *Paradise Lost*, but I try to bring them closer to *thinking* of the poem as I think of it.

    *Paradise Lost* is, surely, the greatest poem in English, but it is not lovable; and Milton is the prickliest of poets, full of what

the Romans called *superbia*. ("As a man, he is antipathetic. . . .
Milton is unsatisfactory," wrote T. S. Eliot, primly but not inac-
curately.[5]) Of other readers of the poem, the one who best
speaks for me is Virginia Woolf when in her diary she writes,

> I am struck by the extreme difference between this poem
> and any other. It lies, I think, in the sublime aloofness and
> impersonality of the emotion. . . . But how smooth, strong
> and elaborate it all is! What poetry! I can conceive that
> even Shakespeare after this would seem a little troubled,
> personal, hot and imperfect. I can conceive that this is the
> essence, of which almost all other poetry is the dilution.[6]

The poem's evident power, coupled with its resistance to any
of the typical approaches we make to poetry, offers endless
fascination; which is why I have sometimes longed to be a
Miltonist. "Iron sharpens iron," says the book of Proverbs, and

5. From Eliot's first essay on Milton (1936), in *On Poetry and Poets* (New York:
Farrar, Straus and Giroux, 1957), p. 156. It is rare to find a reader of Milton who
thinks he would have been enjoyable company, but—even though grappling with
the complexities of Milton's personality is not part of my remit here—I feel that I
should note Christopher Hill's dissent from the usual view in his *Milton and the
English Revolution* (Harmondsworth: Penguin, 1979), p. 78: "It still seems to be
necessary to combat the view that Milton was a gloomy Puritan. This is part of a
general misunderstanding, arising from reading back into the seventeenth century
the characteristics, or alleged characteristics, of nineteenth-century nonconfor-
mity. . . . The 'nonconformist' interpretation is quite inappropriate to Milton, the
poet and musician who regarded elegance as one of the virtues. All who knew him
stressed his 'Very cheerful humour', his 'sweet and affable nature', his 'unaffected
cheerfulness and civility'; he was 'delightful company, the life of the conversation'
and 'very merry.'"

6. Virginia Woolf, *A Writer's Diary: Being Extracts from the Diary of Virginia
Woolf* (San Diego: Harcourt/Harvest, 1982), p. 6.

in reading the works of the great Miltonists I often feel that they have been sharpened to a fine edge by their constant encounters with the unyielding metal of Milton's mind, and with one another. (No group of scholars is sinless, but I have long admired the fierce courtesy with which Miltonists tend to conduct their disputations.) And yet I also feel them responding to something very different, to the Baroque elaboration of his verse, and especially in *Paradise Lost* to its sheer and supreme gorgeousness, like that of a Bernini church. I feel that I learn more from Miltonists than from the critics of any other poet. And so, while freely admitting that I am not among their number, I want to begin by acknowledging my debt to and admiration for them.

# A NOTE ON TEXTS AND
# ABBREVIATIONS

THE AUTHORITATIVE edition of Milton's writings is *The Complete Works of John Milton* in eleven volumes (Oxford University Press), under the general editorship of Thomas N. Corns and Gordon Campbell. In writing this book I have often consulted these volumes, but because they are typically found only in university libraries—or, in digital form, available only to university faculty and students—I cite Milton's works from scholarly but more readily available texts, using the following abbreviations:

- PL = *Paradise Lost,* ed. Alastair Fowler, 2nd ed. (Harlow, Essex: Longman, 1998). All references to the poem are indicated in the text simply by book and line number (e.g., IV.287); use of the abbreviation typically indicates a reference to Fowler's introduction and notes.
- CP = *John Milton: The Complete Poems*, ed. John Leonard (London: Penguin, 1998). This for all poetry by Milton other than *Paradise Lost*.
- PR = *John Milton Prose: Major Writings on Liberty, Politics, Religion, and Education*, ed. David Loewenstein

(Chichester: Wiley-Blackwell, 2013). I have occasionally taken the liberty of modernizing spelling.

Whenever possible and appropriate, I have cited public-domain works in widely accessible editions that have been prepared with scholarly care. Readers who want to know more about the works I have quoted will be find Oxford World's Classics or Penguin Classics versions more readily than those definitive scholarly editions that are available primarily or only in research libraries. In cases in which there are no modern editions—Sir Walter Scott's *Woodstock*, for instance, or Addison's essays on *Paradise Lost*—I have cited chapter numbers or other such division markings in full trust that my readers can and do use Google Books, Project Gutenberg, and the Internet Archive.

# 1

# The Poet

THIS IS the biography of a poem, not a poet; but, as the rest of this book will amply demonstrate, the fate of this poem came to be intricately (and in many instances unfortunately) intertwined with ideas about its author. Often we shall see that when readers respond to *Paradise Lost*—with admiration or disgust—they are responding less to the poem itelf than to the mind they discern behind it. So it is with the curious and controversial career of that author that we must begin.

The ninth book of *Paradise Lost*, the one that describes the Fall of Adam and Eve from the perfect bliss for which they had been created, commences with a plea for divine assistance. This is the poet's third such plea. Milton had begun his poem with an invocation, a double one seeking aid first from the "Heavenly Muse" and then from the Holy Spirit. He had sought aid again at the outset of Book III, calling, as his story made the dramatic transition from the "darkness visible" of Hell to the bright courts of Heaven, for the illumination of "holy light." This plea is followed by a moving description of his blindness:

Gal. Faithorne ad Vivum.                    Delin. et sculpsit.

Joannis Miltoni Effigies Ætat: 62.
1670.

FIGURE 1. John Milton, by William Faithorne (1670).
National Portrait Gallery, London.

Seasons return, but not to me returns
Day, or the sweet approach of Ev'n or Morn,
Or sight of vernal bloom, or Summers Rose,
Or flocks, or herds, or human face divine;
But cloud instead, and ever-during dark
Surrounds me, from the cheerful ways of men
Cut off, and for the Book of knowledge fair
Presented with a Universal blank
Of Nature's works to me expung'd and ras'd,
And wisdom at one entrance quite shut out.
  (III.40–49)

The invocation at the outset of the ninth book grows more personal still, and expresses an uncharacteristic diffidence. After all, Milton says, his topic is one "Not less but more Heroic than the wrath / Of stern Achilles on his Foe pursu'd / Thrice Fugitive about Troy Wall" (IX.14–16); more heroic also than the tales told in the *Odyssey* and even the *Aeneid*. Can he really claim to be adequate to the challenge? Only if he can secure the aid of his "Celestial Patroness," who, he tells us twice within a few lines, comes to him at night and whispers to him in his sleep, or merely "inspires" his "unpremeditated verse"—which is to say, he does not struggle to draft his lines: they come to him "easy," in the night. (And then, we know from other sources, he would next morning dictate them to his amanuenses.)

Still, he's worried. Has he come "an age too late"?—Is the era of true epic poetry gone forever? Or, perhaps, is the "cold / Climate" of England hostile to the Mediterranean muses of his poetic predecessors? Or might his efforts be compromised by the simple yet inevitable effects of old age? (Milton was in his late fifties when he composed these lines, but given the life expectancies in his time and place, and his own history of indifferent health, he had reason to consider himself elderly.)

One thing he is sure of: that his theme is the proper one. Though war had long been "the only Argument"—that is, subject—thought to be truly heroic, he hotly dissents from that judgment, and especially disdains the medieval and early modern poems that describe "Races and Games . . . emblazon'd Shields . . . Caparisons and Steeds . . . gorgeous Knights / At Joust and Tournament" (IX.33–41)—the whole business being, to Milton, a "long and tedious havoc." About all such stuff he says he is "Nor skilled nor studious": he knows little and doesn't care to know more.[1] That said, he admits that he did not quickly come to the choice he now claims to be "higher": His course was one of "long choosing, and beginning late."

But why? Why did he take so long to choose his epic theme, his "great Argument," and still longer to begin listening for the whispered nocturnal words of his Celestial Patroness?

———

Milton was born in London in December of 1608.[2] His father, also John Milton, was a scrivener—a scribe or notary, one paid

1. However, he remained always reverent towards Edmund Spenser, author of the *Faerie Queene* and his chief predecessor as an English poet working on an epic scale. See Christopher Hill, *Milton and the English Revolution*, p. 80, for multiple examples.

2. My knowledge of Milton's life comes primarily from three excellent biographies, those by Barbara K. Lewalski, Gordon Campbell and Thomas N. Corns, and Nicholas McDowell.

to write documents of many sorts—and his office in Bread Street, at the sign of the Spread Eagle, was also the family home. (The Spread Eagle was the traditional sign of a scrivener, so the illiterate—all too often in need of scriveners—could find the person they needed.) But the elder John was by avocation a composer and musician, and from an early age his son was engaged in the family's musical endeavors. About the poet's mother, Sara, we know almost nothing, not even the date of her marriage, though some years after her death her son would write of her, "my mother [was] a woman of purest reputation, celebrated throughout the neighborhood for her acts of charity" (PR 346). The Worshipful Company of Scriveners was (and is) one of the famous livery companies of London, along with the Mercers, the Merchant Taylors, the Vintners, and many others—organized and well-respected professions all.[3] The Miltons were rather well off; not rich, but substantial.

Young John was first educated at home, then at St. Paul's School.[4] Founded in 1509 by the great Renaissance humanist John Colet, it was located just on the north side of St. Paul's Cathedral, while Bread Street lay just south. This was Old St. Paul's, the magnificent Gothic church that would be destroyed in the Great Fire of London in 1666. At school he

3. The addition in recent years of the Worshipful Company of Management Consultants, the Worshipful Company of International Bankers, and the Worshipful Company of Security Professionals has rather altered the tone of the livery-company tradition.

4. In his Latin poem "*Ad Patrem*" ("To His Father") Milton praises the elder John Milton for providing him an excellent education—though there are some hints of paternal frustration at the son's delay in choosing and sticking with a career (CP 573ff).

learned to write English prose, to read and write Latin prose and verse, and then to read a little Greek and (eventually) Hebrew. Later Milton would say that as much as he admired Greek verse, he admired Hebrew verse more, and his earliest surviving poems are English versions of Psalms 114 and 136; Milton thought highly enough of them not just to keep them, but when he was in his thirties to publish them.[5] He said then that he had written them at age fifteen, that is, in 1624.

The year after that he went up to Christ's College, Cambridge—sixteen was not then an unusual age to begin university; his closest friend, Charles Diodati, began Oxford at thirteen—where he had a mixed experience. He wrote many poems, most of them in English, most of them elegies for friends or teachers; but he also wrote in Latin some vigorous anti-Catholic polemics, and late in his time at Cambridge he began to devote serious time and energy to the writing of poems in Italian. To comply with certain requirements, he composed and delivered Latin addresses, known as "Prolusions." He became widely known as "the Lady of Christ's"—he refers jokingly to this in one of his Prolusions—probably

5. In *The Reason of Church Government* (1642) Milton notes "those magnificent odes and hymns wherein Pindarus and Callimachus are in most things worthy," but then asserts that "those frequent songs throughout the law and prophets beyond all these, not in their divine argument alone, but in the very critical art of composition, may be easily made appear over all the kinds of lyric poesy to be incomparable" (PR 89). In *A Preface to "Paradise Lost"* C. S. Lewis comments: "I once had a pupil, innocent alike of the Greek and of the Hebrew tongue, who did not think himself thereby disqualified from pronouncing this judgement a proof of Milton's bad taste; the rest of us, whose Greek is amateurish and who have no Hebrew, must leave Milton to discuss the question with his peers" (pp. 4–5).

because he was a slight and elegant youth with long silky hair;[6] and he was certainly recognized for possessing great gifts.

But he was not happy at Cambridge. He wrote to a London friend in 1628 that he was "finding almost no intellectual companions here," and for the rest of his life he would be contemptuous of what he believed to be the frivolity of university education in Britain. He struggled to get along with his tutor, and some would later say that he was rusticated—expelled for a season—though no surviving records say so. He does seem to have left Cambridge for a period, willingly or unwillingly, but eventually he took his bachelor's degree and later returned for the brief period of residency necessary to gain the master's. After that he spent several years in and near London, reading and studying—it was convenient for him to have a well-fixed father—nominally in preparation for a *sanctae theologiae baccalaureus* (later called the Bachelor of Divinity).

In any case he was glad to be done with Cambridge, and one suspects that he never would have left central London again if his father had not decided to seek a more rural life, first in Hammersmith—a mere hamlet in those days, seven miles from London proper—and later in the village of Horton, then in Buckinghamshire. Milton was a Londoner through and through, and everything that he did and wrote should be understood in that light. That city's character and fortunes always shaped his own.

6. Some Milton scholars have thought it significant that Aelius Donatus, a fourth-century biographer of Virgil, says that when Virgil lived in Naples he was commonly known as the Virgin (*parthenias vulgo appellatus sit*). But "virgin" and "lady" are scarcely synonyms.

In 1609, when Milton was just a few months old, the plague had swept through London. We do not know whether his family left the city at that time, though it was common for those who could afford it to seek refuge in the plague-free countryside. (That year's outbreak may have been the event that led William Shakespeare to end his long residency in the city and return to his hometown of Stratford-upon-Avon.) Waves of the plague would recur in London through Milton's life, and when they did he and his family—first his parents, later his wife and children—would typically make a brief rural retreat. But he would not live outside the city for an extended period until the massive outbreak in 1665 that sent him for some months to Chalfont St. Giles, Buckinghamshire. This season of Milton's life gets more attention than it deserves because he completed *Paradise Lost* there, and because the cottage he occupied still exists and has been turned into a museum, whereas none of his London residences remain—most places associated with Milton, including the house in Bread Street, were destroyed in the Great Fire of 1666. But make no mistake: *Paradise Lost* is a poem conceived by a Londoner, composed largely in London, and published in London. It is one of the definitive documents of that city's spiritual and intellectual life, rivaled in that respect primarily by the visionary poems and prints of William Blake.

And London is the very center of the political turmoil that would dominate the second half of Milton's life—turmoil that would result in the toppling and execution of a king, an event which led to Milton's becoming a government official; that appointment led in turn to his imprisonment as a traitor and the imminent danger of execution. As Roy Porter wrote of this period,

[T]he coming of the new Stuart dynasty, fresh from Scotland and green in English politics, created friction between King and Commons, often over money matters dear to City hearts, such as excise and taxation. It would, recent historians have insisted, be rank hindsight to imply that early Stuart rule was rushing unstoppably down the rapids towards the Niagara of the Civil War, a disaster in which London was destined to be ranged against the King, representing, as vulgar Marxists might put it, bourgeois revolution against feudal monarchy. Nevertheless the metropolis was becoming so populous and powerful, so indispensable to royal solvency and the nation's prosperity, that the days had long passed when the White Tower terrorized the citizenry, or rebel leaders would meekly be led off to Mile End by a Richard II: things soon turned out quite the reverse, with a King being led to the scaffold, ironically in front of Inigo Jones's Banqueting House.[7]

7. Roy Porter, *London: A Social History* (Cambridge: Harvard University Press, 1998), p. 89. Inigo Jones had been commissioned to design and build Banqueting House by Charles's father, King James I. As Porter goes on to show, the financiers of the City did not immediately abandon Charles, and some of them were always ready to lend money to him, but "the turning point came on January 1642, when Charles tried to arrest five House of Commons opponents and they fled into the City, thereby sealing a Parliament/London bond. The king pursued. At the Guildhall his reception was mixed, but in the streets a howling mob of tradesmen, apprentices and mariners cried 'privilege of parliament, privilege of parliament.' . . . In July 1642 the royalist Lord Mayor was impeached in Parliament, dismissed, and clapped in the Tower. A radical was appointed in his place, and London armed for war" (p. 72).

This was Milton's London. He lived and worked there through this period of escalating tension, and would have felt that tension in his bones.

But *his* concerns were not economic, or even, at first, strictly political. He was a learned man, one inclined first to the service of poetry and second to the service of the church; he was neither merchant nor politician. And yet he was gradually drawn into a world of revolution and regicide: of both he became the most famous and eloquent defender. Perhaps the single greatest puzzle about Milton's life is this: When and how was he radicalized? If, like his intimate friend Charles Diodati, he had died at age twenty-eight, he would have been seen as a relatively typical product of his time and social class: an erudite and sophisticated young poet who had shown no interest in politics and had never openly questioned the doctrine and discipline of the Church of England. But in his thirties he became a revolutionary and a defender of regicide. What happened?

In early modern Britain, you would have been hard-pressed to find anyone who believed that questions about the proper character of the state could be divorced from beliefs about the nature of the True Church. In the Elizabethan era a certain equilibrium between church and state had been laboriously achieved, though at the cost, to those who persevered in the Roman faith, of a profound loss of rights and privileges. Roman Catholic worship was legally forbidden throughout England; only those who affirmed the Church of England's Articles of Religion could receive degrees from Oxford or Cambridge; after the Popish Recusants Act of 1605 was passed—in response to the Gunpowder Plot to blow up the Houses of

Parliament—no Catholic could practice law or medicine, or serve as anyone's legal guardian or trustee. But with the succession of King Charles I in 1625, and the increasing power of his favored clergyman William Laud—named Archbishop of Canterbury in 1633—many Protestants came under legal scrutiny from Charles and his clerical servants. To be sure, king and prelates were not necessarily of one mind about all things. Laud's opponents always denigrated him as popish, but he was staunchly opposed to the Roman church; Charles, whose wife, Henrietta Maria, was Catholic and whose mother may have been as well, was less hostile. In any case, the crown and its church prelates became less concerned with any threat coming from Recusants (Catholics who *recused* themselves from Anglican worship services) and more concerned with Presbyterians and other Dissenters (those who *dissented* from some of the Articles of Religion) and Puritans (who remained obedient but sought to *purify* what they believed to be a corrupt Church of England).

This Laudian orthodoxy was much concerned to mandate certain forms of worship and liturgical practice—and to enforce its mandates. This project of administrative surveillance at one point touched the Milton family quite directly. In 1636 the elder Milton resigned from his role in the Company of Scriveners and he and his family moved to the village of Horton, then in Buckinghamshire, where, a year later, Sara Milton died and was buried under the aisle of the parish church. Soon thereafter a Laudian archdeacon, visiting the parish as a representative of the bishop of Lincoln, scrutinized the arrangements. He found some things to his liking and some things not. The rector's surplice was inappropriate, for instance; and the family pew of the Miltons was too high. Moreover, Sara Milton's tombstone was improperly oriented—the inscription faced the wrong way—and the archdeacon ordered it to be reversed. In the event, it was not altered, but we know nothing about the Milton family's feelings on this matter. Did they treat it as the kind of minor annoyance that inevitably accompanies interactions with bureaucracy? Or were they more deeply offended? No evidence tells us.

We know that when Milton was at Cambridge he made all of the requisite affirmations of the principles that would ultimately be called Laudian; he also tells us that from an early age his family intended him for the church and that (as noted earlier) he studied towards a Bachelor of Divinity degree through much of the 1630s. But the greatest of his early poems, "Lycidas," written in 1637, departs briefly from its elegiac mood to utter a fierce denunciation of clerical corruption. ("Blind mouths! that scarce themselves know how to hold / A sheephook, or have learn'd aught else the least / That to the faithful herdman's art belongs!" [CP 44]) And very soon after he returned from his Italian journey in 1638 and 1639 he began to write antiprelatical pamphlets—pamphlets denouncing what he believed to be an excess of priestly authority over the Christian people of England. How he got from affirmation to denunciation is simply not known, though speculation has been endless among Miltonists.

He himself put the matter simply. In *The Reason of Church Government* (1642) he responds to the argument that, as a layman, he has no business arguing about how the church should be structured. He says that he had long felt the proper Christian impulse to aid "the church, to whose service by the intentions of my parents and friends I was destined of a child, and in mine own resolutions"; but then, "coming to some maturity of years and perceiving what tyranny had invaded the church, that he who would take orders must subscribe slave, and take an oath withal, which unless he took with a conscience that would retch, he must either straight perjure or split his faith," he decided to refrain from ordination. It is better to practice "a blameless silence" than to acquire "the sacred office of speaking bought and begun with servitude and forswearing." Yet would such silence not be a lamentable refusal "to help ease and lighten the difficult labors of the church"? Thus, in the end, having been "church-outed by the prelates"—denied the possibility of honest ministry by arrogant and tyrannical Laudians—he decided that "God by his secretary conscience" required him to speak anyway (PR 91). He makes no mention, here or elsewhere, of being moved by any personal affront. No argument from silence can be definitive, but Milton was not one to ignore a slight.[8]

Writing more than a decade later, in 1654, when he was serving in Oliver Cromwell's government, Milton responded to some of his many critics by saying that everything he wrote in the 1640s was done in service to a single overarching principle: the defense of liberty.

I observed that there are, in all, three varieties of liberty without which civilized life is scarcely possible, namely

---

8. In his *Second Defense* he bristles at personal insults flung at him by his opponents: "Ugly I have never been thought by anyone, to my knowledge, who has laid eyes on me. . . . I admit that I am not tall, but my stature is closer to the medium than to the small. . . . Although I am past forty, there is scarcely anyone to whom I do not seem younger by about ten years" (PR 334).

ecclesiastical liberty, domestic or personal liberty, and civil liberty, and since I had already written about the first, while I saw that the magistrates were vigorously attending to the third, I took as my province the remaining one, the second or domestic kind. This too seemed to be concerned with three problems: the nature of marriage itself, the education of the children, and finally the existence of freedom to express oneself. Hence I set forth my views of marriage, not only its proper contraction, but also, if need be, its dissolution. (PR 349)

In 1642 Milton, age thirty-three, married seventeen-year-old Mary Powell, but after just a few weeks of marriage she returned to her parents. Eventually she was convinced to rejoin her husband, but Milton had already begun a massive project of research into what he would call *The Doctrine and Discipline of Divorce* (the title of the first of four lengthy tracts he would publish between 1643 and 1645)—essentially looking for ways to evade the evident bluntness of Jesus's declaration that a man cannot divorce his wife except on the grounds of her "fornication" (Matthew 19).

Milton's description of these tracts is puzzling. He wrote, "Concerning this matter then I published several books, at the very time when man and wife were often bitter foes, he dwelling at home with their children, she, the mother of the family, in the camp of the enemy, threatening her husband with death and disaster" (PR 349). This reference to the English Civil War, then raging, is either allegorical—civil war figured as a divorce—or an example of a legitimate cause for seeking divorce, i.e., you may divorce your wife if she wants you murdered. It's impossible to tell, and one cannot but suspect an evasiveness in his account of the divorce tracts. He does not in any event mention his own marital struggles.

And as he continues to describe his writing of those years he returns to an emphasis on themes of general relevance:

> Next, in one small volume, I discussed the education of children, a brief treatment to be sure, but sufficient, as I thought, for those who devote to the subject the attention it deserves. For nothing can be more efficacious than education in moulding the minds of men to virtue (whence arises true and internal liberty), in governing the state effectively, and preserving it for the longest possible space of time. (PR 350)

This is a reference to his famous essay "Of Education" (1644); though for a time in the 1630s he has been a tutor to his sister's children and eventually to a few others, he ignores that experience here and reaffirms his concern for preserving and protecting liberty. And he continues along these lines:

> Lastly I wrote, on the model of a genuine speech, the *Areopagitica*, concerning freedom of the press, that the judgment of truth and falsehood, what should be printed and what suppressed, ought not to be in the hands of a few men (and these mostly ignorant and of vulgar discernment) charged with the inspection of books, at whose will or whim virtually everyone is prevented from publishing aught that surpasses the understanding of the mob.[9]

9. It should be noted here that, though Milton has gone down in history as the great proponent of "freedom of the press," he explicitly says in *Areopagitica* that no Catholic writings should be licensed: "I mean not tolerated Popery, and open

Thus Milton denies that any of his varied prose works of the 1640s—whether on the power of prelates, or the circumstances under which a marriage may be ended, or the nature of education, or the licensing of printed documents—are responses to his own circumstances. They are, rather, disinterested (if not dispassionate) defenses of one great overarching principle.

The reader is free to decide whether or not to believe him. But there is no question that Milton did have an unusually high regard for liberty; and there seems to have been a very particular reason for that. I have already referred to the passage from his *Reason of Church Government* in which Milton defends his participation, as a layman, in ecclesiastical debates; but it is a passage worth returning to, because it is revelatory in several ways. His status as a layman is not the only factor that might disqualify Milton from engagement in the debate, he acknowledges; his youth also, his "green years," count against him. Anticipating this criticism, Milton embarks on a sinuous train of reasoning. First, "the elegant and learned reader" will, surely, understand that Milton does not seek praise for his polemics, because if *that* was what he wanted, "I should not write thus out of mine own season, when I have [not] yet completed to my mind the full circle of my private studies." His chief point here is that one of "green years" who leaps into such a fray must be in earnest (though it's noteworthy

---

superstition, which as it extirpates all religions and civil supremacies, so itself should be extirpate, provided first that all charitable and compassionate means be used to win and regain the weak and the misled: that also which is impious or evil absolutely either against faith or manners no law can possibly permit, that intends not to unlaw itself" (PR 211). Of course, every text banned by every government is deemed "evil absolutely."

that more than a decade after taking his Master of Arts, Milton still feels his education inadequate to his ambitions). However, this admission should not be taken to indicate that he's not up to the current challenge: "I complain not of any insufficiency to the matter in hand." Indeed, the task is so easy that if Milton had *chosen* it, that would have led to "knowing my self inferior to my self," a kind of self-betrayal. In refuting the prelates and their supporters, "I have the use, as I may account it, but of my left hand"—the task is so easily accomplished that he has no need of the stronger right one (PR 88).

But this only raises a question: What are the ambitions to which his education has been inadequate? What kind of task *would* require the use of both hands? Why, the writing of *great poetry*, of course. He finds himself "sitting here below in the cool element of prose," when he would, given his choice, be "a Poet soaring in the high region of his fancies with his garland and singing robes about him." The learned scholars and poets he met on his recent voyage to Italy told him that he was capable of becoming such a poet; and

> I began this far to assent both to them and divers of my friends here at home, and not less to an inward prompting which now grew daily upon me, that by labour and intent study (which I take to be my portion in this life) joined with the strong propensity of nature, I might perhaps leave something so written to after times, as they should not willingly let it die. (PR 88)

(That is beautifully said.) So why not take up that poetic work, if indeed it is his calling, rather than engage in these one-armed polemics?

This question takes us to the nub of the matter. Milton considers what a government is for, and affirms that "it were happy for the Commonwealth, if our Magistrates, as in those famous governments of old, would take into their care, not only the deciding of our contentious law cases and brawls," but also the education of the people in virtue—and for Milton that means the promotion of proper entertainments and arts, leisure activities that

> may civilize, adorn and make discreet our minds by the learned and affable meeting of frequent Academies, and the procurement of wise and artful recitations sweetened with eloquent and graceful enticements to the love and practice of justice, temperance and fortitude, instructing and bettering the Nation at all opportunities, that the call of wisdom and virtue may be heard everywhere. (PR 90)

(Remember also his belief, articulated in his essay "Of Education," that virtue is the guarantor of liberty.) It is to this cause that Milton believes himself as a poet to be called: "to be an interpreter and relater of the best and sagest things among mine own Citizens throughout this island in the mother dialect"—"those intentions . . . have liv'd within me ever since I could conceive myself any thing worth to my Country" (PR 91). His only *true* ambition, then, had been to become the English Virgil, the author of the English *Aeneid*.

But the current Magistrates are too occupied by "contentious law cases and brawls"; by inferior schemes of education; by intrusive overpolicing of printing and of church ceremonies and of the placement of tombstones in churches, to take up the noble cause of "instructing and bettering the Nation." They not only fail to encourage and support the arts, they, through their constraints upon liberty, actively impede the ability of artists like Milton to fulfill their vocations. Such vocations can be fulfilled only when England has "enfranchised herself from this impertinent yoke of prelaty"; because "under [such] inquisitorious and tyrannical duncery no free and splendid wit can flourish" (PR 91). So, until that yoke is lifted, that duncery banished, true liberty restored, Milton must set aside his garland and singing robes, and must write cold prose with his left hand.[10]

So began his career as a polemicist and, later, a government official. From his early thirties to his early fifties, Milton rarely donned those robes. When, in 1646, in the midst of a barrage of pamphlets, he published *Poems of Mr. John Milton*, he must have felt that he was remembering another life. A year later his father died and he gave up teaching; in 1649, just weeks after Charles I was tried and executed by Parliament, he published *The Tenure of Kings and Magistrates*, an argument that rulers only rule on behalf of and at the sufferance of the People. This led immediately to his appointment as Secretary for Foreign Tongues to the Commonwealth Council of State, a position he held until the Commonwealth government ended with the restoration of the monarchy in 1660.[11] Later in 1649 he

10. This is the great emphasis of Nicholas McDowell's biography, *Poet of Revolution: The Making of John Milton* (Princeton: Princeton University Press, 2020): "Milton's political development is shaped by his evolving understanding of the ways in which 'tyranny'—defined initially in ecclesiastical and clerical terms but which grows to encompass political organization—retards the intellectual and cultural progress of a nation" (p. 13).

11. Essentially, Milton was responsible for communicating with other European governments, usually in Latin. Two of his colleagues were Andrew Marvell and

published *Eikonoklastes,* a passionate defense of the execution of Charles, whom some were already beginning to think of as King Charles the Martyr.

In the next decade Milton helped conduct foreign affairs for the government, and wrote more polemical treatises defending the execution of the king and celebrating the Commonwealth as a restorer of true liberty; he also began work on a history of England. His wife Mary died, and his young son John; he married again, but within a year and a half his wife and infant daughter, both named Katherine, also died. (His three daughters from his first marriage, Anne, Mary, and Deborah, survived.) Having long had poor eyesight, he became completely blind.[12] In early 1660, just before King Charles II came to assume his throne and therefore far too late, he wrote one last political treatise, this one explaining how a commonwealth might be established and sustained.

All of his political and most of his personal hopes had been dashed. If under the Commonwealth true liberty has

---

John Dryden: thus the three greatest English poets of the age worked together as bureaucrats, possibly even sharing an office, though because of his blindness Milton worked mainly at home. Surely this is a unique circumstance.

12. His enemies thought his blindness a sign of God's judgment against him. To this, in his *Second Defense,* he replied, "Your blindness, deeply implanted in the inmost faculties, obscures the mind, so that you may see nothing whole or real. Mine, which you make a reproach, merely deprives things of color and superficial appearance. What is true and essential in them is not lost to my intellectual vision. . . . Nor do I feel pain at being classed with the blind, the afflicted, the suffering, and the weak (although you hold this to be wretched), since there is hope that in this way I may approach more closely the mercy and protection of the Father Almighty. There is a certain road which leads through weakness, as the apostle teaches, to the greatest strength" (PR 335).

been gained, in the Restoration it was surely lost again. Two of his books were banned and burned, and he was arrested and imprisoned.[13] As not merely a supporter of the Commonwealth but one of its leading officers, and the single most uncompromising advocate for the execution of the father of the new king, he had every reason to expect to be publicly and brutally executed. Instead, for reasons unknown, he was released.[14]

It was time, he decided, to place a garland upon his head, to don his robes, and to sing.

13. The burning of the books—*Eikonoklastes* and the *Second Defense*—was largely symbolic; no attempt was made to confiscate copies. Book burners had learned a lot in the century and a half since the Bishop of London bought up all the copies he could find of William Tyndale's translation of the New Testament and burned them in a great auto-da-fé. Tyndale took all the money he made from the transaction and used it to print a new edition, with corrections and revisions.

14. The standard form of execution of a traitor required him to be hanged, but not until dead: he was to be cut down while still living to have his sexual organs amputated, to have his entrails torn from his abdomen and burned before his eyes, and only then to be beheaded and bodily divided into four quarters. See Barbara K. Lewalski, *The Life of John Milton: A Critical Biography*, rev. ed. (Oxford: Blackwell, 2003), p. 400. Speculation about why Milton was spared is infinite and infinitely inconclusive, but the most likely explanation is that the new government thought it adequate to destroy the man's books in place of the man himself. It may well be that this course of action was recommended by Andrew Marvell, who by this time was a Member of Parliament—though he had been Milton's colleague, he somehow managed to avoid condemnation by the new regime. And Milton had other friends among royalists. A final factor: It is quite possible, as Gordon Campbell and Thomas N. Corns argue in *John Milton: Life, Work, and Thought* (Oxford: Oxford University Press, 2008), p. 309, that the new government believed that Milton could be persuaded to use his powerful rhetorical and argumentative gifts on its behalf.

# 2

# The Poem

SING HE did; though not the song he had once, long before,
expected to sing.

After Milton's death, a collection of his papers was bound
into a single volume that we now call the Trinity manuscript, because it is housed in the Wren Library of Trinity
College, Cambridge.[1] The papers all concern poetry, and
though Milton never bound them, it seems that he kept his
poetic drafts and ideas together, and separate from his polemical prose. The first entries in the manuscript, from the
early 1630s, are drafts of poems, including his greatest
shorter poem, "Lycidas"; the later entries, made after Milton
had gone blind, are in the handwriting of his various secretaries and amanuenses. Of particular interest for our purposes are seven pages—written in the months after Milton's

---

1. The complete manuscript may be viewed at the library's website: https://mss
-cat.trin.cam.ac.uk/Manuscript/R.3.4/UV#?c=0&m=0&s=0&cv=0&r=0&xywh
=-1721%2C-214%2C6027%2C4246. The pages I discuss here are reproduced in
PL 1–2.

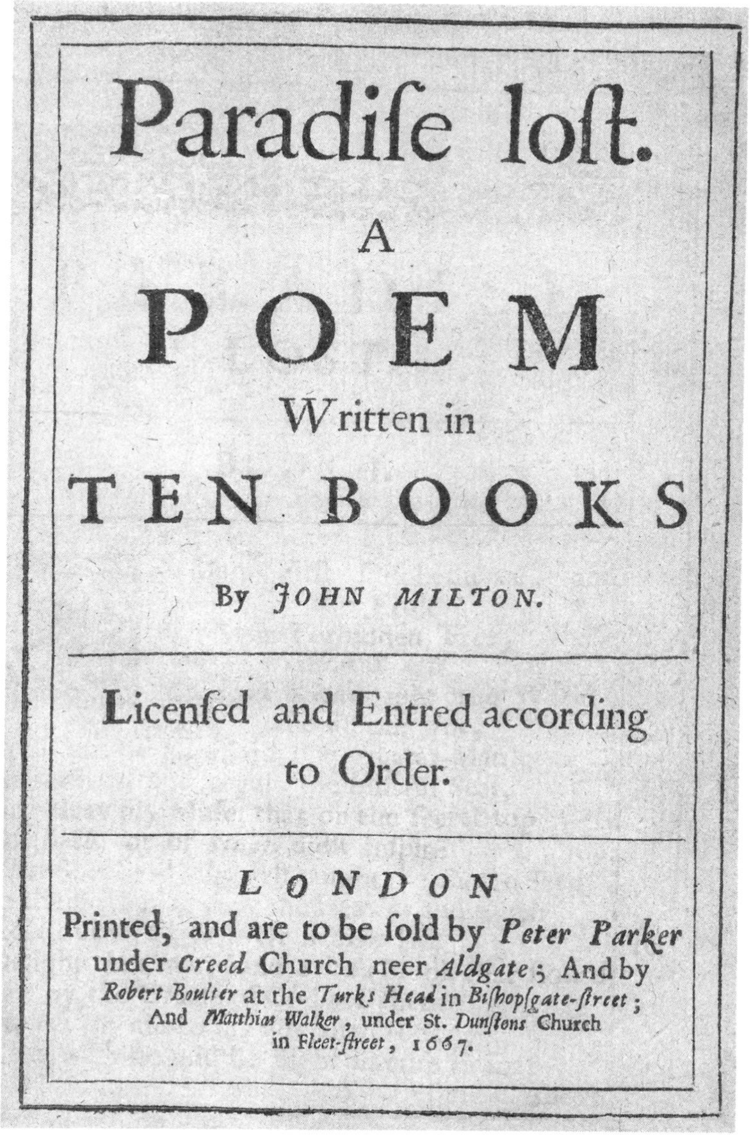

# Paradiſe loſt.

## A

# POEM

### Written in

# TEN BOOKS

#### By JOHN MILTON.

Licenſed and Entred according
to Order.

### LONDON

Printed, and are to be ſold by *Peter Parker*
under *Creed* Church neer *Aldgate* ; And by
*Robert Boulter* at the *Turks Head* in *Biſhopſgate-ſtreet* ;
And *Matthias Walker*, under St. *Dunſtons* Church
in *Fleet-ſtreet*, 1 6 6 7.

FIGURE 2. Title page of the first edition of *Paradise Lost*, before
Milton divided the poem into twelve books and prefaced each book
with an Argument.

return from Italy but before the commencement of his polemical career—of ideas for possible poems. For instance,
Milton thinks that there is epic potential in certain events
from the reign of King Alfred the Great (848–99). He had
earlier considered an Arthurian subject but came to think
that it was not sufficiently grounded in history—one of his
key authorities, the Italian poet Tasso, had insisted that the
true epic subject must deal with historical events. But most
of the ideas involve drama, especially tragedy: under the
heading "British Trag." he lists thirty-three events that could
serve as suitable subjects.

He also lists a number of biblical topics, including the story
of Samson and various scenes from the life of Christ, but
writes most extensively about four: John the Baptist, Abraham, the destruction of Sodom, and what he first calls "Paradise Lost" and then, later, "Adam unparadiz'd." Sketches for
the first three look like five-act tragedies in the Roman mold;
but the fourth one is more formally peculiar: he doesn't seem
to know quite how to tell the story of the Fall. Even when he
outlines it in five acts he includes allegorical personages, figures that seem to be refugees from a medieval morality play:
in one sketch he has Justice, Mercy, and Wisdom "debating
what should become of man if he fall"; in an earlier outline
characters include Conscience and Death.

The idea of a great work on biblical themes was a common
one in Milton's time. In the previous century the Italian poet
Marco Girolama Vida had written the *Christiad* (1535), a poem
in six books on the life of Jesus. Milton's near-contemporary
Abraham Cowley—much celebrated in his own day, though by
the 1730s Alexander Pope would be asking, "Who now reads

Cowley?"[2]—worked for many years, first in Latin and then in English, on an epic poem about the life of King David, but left the *Davideis* unfinished. There was perhaps particular interest in the book of Genesis, which, as Arnold Williams reminds us, played an absolutely central role in the imagination of the early modern period, for which "Moses was . . . the first historian, the first poet, even the first author; and the book of Genesis was his first work, and consequently the first literary production in history."[3] This centrality led Lucy Hutchinson—the same age as Cowley, a decade younger than Milton—to produce in 1679 a book-length verse paraphrase, in heroic couplets: *Order and Disorder: Or, The World Made and Undone. Being Meditations upon the Creation and the Fall; As it is recorded in the beginning of Genesis.* Such subjects were clearly in the air.

If we turn our gaze to Milton some twenty years after the Trinity manuscript, we see how things have sorted themselves out in his mind. The first point to note is that he has abandoned the idea of writing a poem about his own country. His dreams for a government that will uphold liberty have died; the "inquisitorious and tyrannical duncery" has returned, and under its rule no compelling poetic depiction of civic and personal virtue is possible. If Milton ever renounced the view that "no free and splendid wit can flourish" under such rule, he didn't say so; but if he could not flourish, he could still compose; he

2. In his "Imitations of Horace": "Who now reads Cowley? if he pleases yet, / His moral pleases, not his pointed wit."

3. Arnold Williams, *The Common Expositor: An Account of the Commentators on Genesis, 1527–1633* (Chapel Hill: University of North Carolina Press, 1948), p. 3. Williams's book remains essential for students of Milton, but also offers excellent instruction in how scholars of the early modern period read Genesis.

could still sing. And what he sang, first, was "Adam unparadiz'd." If as a young man he had thought of biblical subjects for the genre of tragedy and national subjects for the genre of epic, now he thinks *only* of biblical subjects.

He worked on the poem that he came to call *Paradise Lost* over a period of roughly five years, though he may have begun work as early as 1658. In the mornings he recited to various amanuenses what, if we are to believe his account, his "Celestial patroness" whispered to him in the night—though, confirmed both his widow and a friend, only in fall and winter ("from the *Autumnal Equinoctial* to the *Vernal*"). As Barbara Lewalski wryly notes, "Given Milton's lifelong fear that a cold climate might hamper high poetic accomplishment"—an anxiety we have seen in our brief look at the beginning of Book IX of the poem—"the Muse's behavior in this regard probably surprised him."[4] During the uninspired seasons of the years in which he was composing *Paradise Lost*, Milton probably spent most of his time working on a big book that he called *De Doctrina Christiana (On Christian Doctrine)*—a title he borrowed from St. Augustine, though Augustine's book is a brief guide to proper reading and interpretation of Scripture, while Milton's is an attempt at a systematic theology.[5]

4. Lewalski, *The Life*, p. 411.

5. It is not certain that Milton is the author of *De Doctrina Christiana*. The book was never published, and exists in a single unsigned manuscript, discovered in 1823. There are, I believe, strong reasons for treating the book as Milton's own and identifying the manuscript with a big theological project that we know, on the basis of contemporary evidence, Milton was working on in the first half of the 1660s. For those interested in exploring the question, an extended debate was conducted in the pages of the journal *Studies in English Literature*, beginning with William B.

Long and productive scholarly careers have been devoted
to teasing out the relationship between the arguments of *De
Doctrina Christiana* and the implicit or explicit theology of
*Paradise Lost*.[6] After all, many have reasoned, it would be odd
indeed if Milton were working on two books simultaneously
that articulated different theologies. But perhaps it would not
be so odd—not for John Milton.

Attempts to place Milton on the maps of seventeenth-century
British religion have always been fraught. He did not believe
that the church should be led by bishops, that's certain; and
though he once made an argument for a presbyterian model
of church governance as the one best supported by the biblical
evidence, he also was scornful about the tendency of British
Presbyterians, once they got into power, to reinvent themselves as prelates. ("New *Presbyter* is but old *Priest* writ large."[7])
He often associated, especially in his later life, with Quakers,
though it seems highly unlikely that Milton was ever in any
sense a Quaker himself. Nicholas McDowell argues that "his
friendships and associations were with men whom he respected

---

Hunter's "The Provenance of the *Christian Doctrine*" (*Studies in English Literature,
1500–1900* 32, no. 1, The English Renaissance [Winter, 1992]: 129–42), and continuing for several years.

6. This tradition began with Maurice Kelley's *This Great Argument: A Study of
Milton's "De Doctrina Christiana" as a Gloss upon "Paradise Lost"* (Princeton: Princeton University Press, 1941).

7. "On the New Forcers of Conscience under the Long Parliament," written
probably in 1646: CP 87. The idea that Milton himself would have become a tyrant
if he had ever held power is a common one among his enemies, and provides the
primary impetus for Peter Ackroyd's 1997 novel *Milton in America*, which imagines
the poet emigrating from England to America at the Restoration and, instead of
writing *Paradise Lost*, ruling despotically over a colony.

for their learning and their appreciation of the 'beautiful,' regardless of their religious allegiances," and this is probably true, though it tells us little about Milton's other beliefs.[8]

Milton has often been called a Puritan, though I think that designation is more misleading than helpful. He was certainly never a Calvinist. So what was he? One contemporary critic spoke derisively of those who accepted Milton's arguments about the permissibility of divorce as "Miltonists," and I think the most accurate thing you can say about Milton's theology is that he was the first Miltonist.[9] In the Epistle that prefaces *De Doctrina Christiana*, Milton writes, "It was . . . evident to me, that, in religion as in other things, the offers of God were all directed, not to an indolent credulity, but to constant diligence, and to an unwearied search after truth." But how does one make this unwearied search? By consulting the Bible:

> For my own part, I adhere to the Holy Scriptures alone; I follow no other heresy or sect. I had not even read any of the works of heretics, so called, when the mistakes of those who are reckoned for orthodox, and their incautious handling of Scripture, first taught me to agree with their opponents whenever those opponents agreed with Scripture. (CP 474)

One searches for truth in the Scriptures, and one searches without the aid of others:

> so far from recommending or imposing anything on my own authority, it is my particular advice that every one

8. McDowell, *Poet of Revolution*, p. 410.
9. McDowell, *Poet of Revolution*, p. 6.

should suspend his opinion on whatever points he may not
feel himself fully satisfied, till the evidence of Scripture pre-
vail, and persuade his reason into assent and faith. (CP 473)

This is what it means to be a Miltonist: not to hold any particular set of beliefs but rather to seek to please God by constantly searching the Scriptures, attending to them and to
them only, and listening always for the voice of conscience,
which as he says elsewhere is "God's secretary," to guide you
in the proper path. Milton cares less about the theological
conclusions one reaches than about the following of this rigor-
ous spiritual and intellectual discipline.

That is why I say it would not necessarily be peculiar or
even surprising if the theology of De Doctrina Christiana dif-
fered in certain respects from that of Paradise Lost—even if we
see the theology of the prose work as internally consistent,
which I doubt that we should do: as Alastair Fowler remarks,
"That [Milton's] theology went through many changes is
reflected in De Doctrina, which should be regarded as an unfinished work in progress" (PL 40). That too would be char-
acteristically Miltonian. For these reasons, I will not in what
follows attempt to use De Doctrina Christiana to elucidate the
theology of Paradise Lost. The poem is its own project of theological inquiry, and should be allowed to speak for itself.

———

The depth and richness, the intricate complexity, of Paradise
Lost make it a difficult work to talk about in a succinct way;
but so I must. Because the purpose of this book is to provide

a biography of the poem—that is, to narrate how it has lived over the centuries since its composition—in describing the poem here I will confine myself to the three major themes or topics that would dominate the poem's post-Milton future: government, sexual politics, and theology proper—*theos + logos*, words about God. All of these topics are, for Milton, in the fullest sense religious; they would be so for many, if not all, of his later readers as well. The narrowing of "religion" as a concept is one of the developments I must account for in the coming pages. This confinement means that certain topics that had major importance to Milton and that I myself find utterly fascinating—for instance, the astronomical and cosmological elements of *Paradise Lost*—will find no place here. I bid them a regretful farewell.

It will thus be necessary to provide a simplified account of the poem's structure—simplified and distorted, distorted to reflect the future life of the poem, what its later readers found compelling (or disgusting) about it. This account will certainly not treat all that Milton himself would have thought essential.

In the narrowest sense, *Paradise Lost* retells the events of the third chapter of Genesis, which narrates briefly and simply a handful of events: The serpent ("more subtle than any beast of the field") persuades Eve to eat the fruit of the one tree in the Garden of Eden that the Lord has forbidden to her and Adam—forbidden on pain of death. The serpent achieves this by convincing her that she will not die but rather will become wise. Eve eats, and gives the fruit to Adam, who also eats. Then they realize that they are naked and are ashamed. The Lord confronts them, issues curses upon Adam, Eve, and the serpent, and expels the couple from the Garden of Eden. The

whole tale is accomplished in about 700 English words, and—
as is typical with stories in the Hebrew Bible, notable, as Erich
Auerbach argued long ago, for their extreme "reticence"[10]—
leaves us with many questions. It is Milton's self-assigned task
to answer them, which he does in many ways, but first by
expanding the scope of his inquiry: this grows to encompass
the first two books of Genesis, then the whole Bible, then the
complete cosmic context. All this will be described below.

At its first publication, in 1667, his poetic tale was divided into
ten books; when it was republished in 1674 ten became twelve—
the same number of books as the *Aeneid*—and many interpret-
ers of the book have worked assiduously to tease out the
numerological significance of these divisions, and of many other
numbers in the poem. All that too will need to be set aside here.
I prefer to see the poem as a series of musical movements:

- Books I–III: Hell and Heaven (*Andante, Presto*)
- Books IV–VIII: The New World and the Old (*Allegro*)
- Book IX: The Great Tragedy (*Largo maestoso*)
- Books X–XII: Aftermath (*Andante*)

10. Erich Auerbach, *Mimesis: The Representation of Reality in Western Literature*,
trans. W. R. Trask (Princeton: Princeton University Press, 1953): "the [biblical]
stories are not, like Homer's, simply narrated 'reality.' Doctrine and promise are
incarnate in them and inseparable from them; for that very reason they are fraught
with 'background' and mysterious, containing a second, concealed meaning. In the
story of Isaac, it is not only God's intervention at the beginning and the end, but
even the factual and psychological elements which come between, that are mysterious, merely touched upon, fraught with background; and therefore they require
subtle investigation and interpretation, they demand them. Since so much in the
story is dark and incomplete, and since the reader knows that God is a hidden God,
his effort to interpret it constantly finds something new to feed upon" (p. 15).

This is an idea with a long and noble pedigree: the original title of John Dryden's *The State of Innocence*—an opera based on *Paradise Lost*—was *The Fall of Angels and Man in Innocence: An Heroic Opera*—and the operatic character of Milton's poem would be recognized and exploited in the twentieth century by Krzysztof Penderecki, a topic we will return to in chapter 6. My own proceeding here, however, as the above description indicates, discerns a musical structure less like that of an opera and more like that of a late Beethoven string quartet.

And so we begin.

———

## Tuning of Instruments; First Movement (*Adagio, Presto*)

Any epic poem tells only a part, if the crucial part, of a larger story. The Trojan War could be said to have begun with the Judgment of Paris—since that decision led to the abduction of Helen, which in turn set all the other dominos falling—and to have ended when the city fell. But Homer chooses to describe the events of just a few days, from Achilles's withdrawal from the fighting to the burial of Hector, breaker of horses. Similarly, the history of Rome is a very long one—in the highest imaginings of the Romans, one not to end until the world itself does—but in the *Aeneid* Virgil narrates for us only the brief period between Aeneas's arrival at Carthage and his defeat of the Rutulian warrior Turnus. But whatever story any given epic strictly tells, the complete arc is always gestured towards, invoked in some way. Thus Aeneas when visiting the underworld sees a vast panorama of the glorious Roman future; and early in the *Iliad* Hector has a grief-stricken vision of the fall of Troy and the enslavement of his beloved wife, Andromache.

The complete story of which *Paradise Lost* is a part may be described thus: God the Father creates; Satan tempts; Adam and Eve fall; the son of God redeems. That arc is never far from Milton's mind in *Paradise Lost*, nor should it be from ours. Thomas Ellwood, a Quaker friend of Milton's, after reading the poem, told him, "Thou has said much here of *Paradise lost*, but what hast thou to say of *Paradise found*?"—and boasted that Milton later said that this comment had been the inspiration for the "brief epic" *Paradise Regained*.[11] In fact, though, the work of the Son to heal and save and redeem and restore is woven into the story of *Paradise Lost* from first to last. It is mentioned in the fourth line of the poem.

But, like those other epics I have mentioned, *Paradise Lost* has a narrower chronological frame, usually said to be vague, though Alastair Fowler, the poem's best editor, believes that the narrative covers precisely thirty-three days.[12] It begins of course in the middle of things, and I think the initial event of the poem is the tumbling of the defeated rebel angels through

11. Campbell and Corns, *John Milton*, p. 328.

12. PL 31. It is obvious where the story *ends*—with the expulsion of Adam and Eve from the Garden of Eden—but where does it *begin*? Fowler is surely correct to say that it begins with the generation of the Son, described in Book V: "This day I have begot whom I declare / My only Son," says the Father (V.603ff). It is this begetting that *immediately* prompts a response in Satan: "fraught / With envy against the Son of God, that day / Honoured by his great Father, and proclaimed / Messiah, King Anointed, could not bear, / Through pride, that sight, and thought himself impaired" (V. 661–65). From there the story unfolds with a certain inevitability.

empty space—the middle of things indeed for them, who have been "Hurled headlong flaming from the ethereal sky / With hideous ruin and combustion down / To bottomless perdition" (I.45ff). While their perdition may be bottomless, their literal descent is not: after "nine times the space that measures day and night / To mortal men" they land with a crash on the floor of their new habitation, Hell. They take some time to recover themselves; Satan is the first to recover and the first to speak, and with his first speech begins the initial movement of the story, the movement during which the fallen rebel angels assess their situation and consider the possibilities for next actions.

They decide, at the urging of Satan, to continue their rebellion, though to continue it not by force of arms but through some deceptive stratagem—what Dante had called *froda* (fraud, deceit) as opposed to *forza*. Satan volunteers for a reconnaissance mission to discover the character of the Almighty's new creation, Man. Not incidentally, Satan is perfectly willing to refer to his conqueror as the Almighty (I.144ff), because this is simply an acknowledgment of strength; he however does *not* acknowledge his conqueror as his creator—in later conversation with an angel, one of his former colleagues, he explicitly denies that God created him or indeed that anyone created him: he claims that he is "self-begot" (V.860).

It is impossible for any informed reader of the story at this point not to remember that Milton, like Satan, rebelled against a king whom he believed to hold a throne not by right but by power. Some have therefore discerned a fundamental inconsistency in *Paradise Lost*, or a reason to think that "Milton was of the devil's party"—more about this phrase in a later chapter—but there is no inconsistency. To say that one king is a tyrant or usurper is not to say that all kings are; in his *Second Defense* Milton says bluntly that he "uttered no word against kings, but only against tyrants" (PR 343). For Milton, a primary task of political thought is to discern (a) what is the legitimate "tenure of kings and magistrates" and what illegitimate, (b) how best to overthrow a regime in which power is illegitimate, and (c) how to create a Commonwealth in which power is justly held. Milton, after laborious and tireless study of Scripture, concludes that God's monarchy is indeed legitimate, and he says it is the task of *Paradise Lost* to defend that conclusion. This is what he means by his famous claim that his purpose is "to justify the ways of God to men" (I.26). Theological reflection and argument can pursue many ends and theodicy is only one of them, but it is the one that Milton says he wishes to achieve.

The primary reason that the ways of God require justification is easily identified: when God the Father could have destroyed Satan and the other rebel angels, he chose not to, and instead allowed Satan to come to this newly created earth and tempt these newly created creatures, made in God's image, to their ruin. And it would be hard to deny that such behavior requires justification. But this is a nettle Milton boldly grasps: just two hundred lines into the poem he writes,

> So stretched out huge in length the Arch-Fiend lay,
> Chained on the burning lake; nor ever thence
> Had risen, or heaved his head, but that the will
> And high permission of all-ruling Heaven
> Left him at large to his own dark designs,
> That with reiterated crimes he might
> Heap on himself damnation, while he sought

Evil to others, and enraged might see
How all his malice served but to bring forth
Infinite goodness, grace, and mercy, shewn
On Man by him seduced, but on himself
Treble confusion, wrath, and vengeance poured.
   (I.209–20)

(This is only part of the sentence that, Brian Cummings notes, is the longest in a poem filled with long sentences.[13]) A small fraction of the way into the poem and the work of justification has already begun—but in a way that acknowledges and faces the strongest challenge that can be brought against God: that he could have averted our misery but chose not to.

So the challenge of theodicy is presented to readers early and often in the poem, and just as we are never allowed to forget that a successful project of redemption is coming— that indeed is part of the work of theodicy—we are also always encouraged to notice through Milton's narration of the events surrounding the fall the ways in which those events in themselves demonstrate the righteousness of "heaven's matchless king," as Satan in a brief weak moment acknowledges him to be (IV.41).

Satan returns from his reconnaissance mission to "this pendant world" (II.1052) to report that these new creatures are ripe for the plucking, and—when no other among the fallen angels volunteers—takes on the task himself, with the result that: "Towards him they bend / With awful reverence prone,

---

13. Brian Cummings, *The Literary Culture of the Reformation: Grammar and Grace* (Oxford: Oxford University Press, 2002), p. 422.

and as a God / Extol him equal to the Highest in Heaven"
(II.479). Before this he had merely been their general; now he
becomes their deity. He thus gets what he had always thought
rightly his—he has now achieved permanently what he had
early assumed for a time: he is, as Milton puts it with savage
wit, "by merit raised / To that bad eminence" (II.5ff).

Thus the first theme of the first movement (*Adagio*) ends
and the second theme (*Presto*) begins—this one trading the
dismal "darkness visible" of Hell for the glorious brightness of
Heaven's courts. Now, finally, the Almighty gets to speak on
his own behalf—in, as it were, his own defense. He speaks
forcefully but juridically, as though waiving questions of abstract Righteousness and focusing instead on the limits of his
legal liability for the unfortunate situation about to unfold. He
has granted to Adam and Eve this lavish accommodation,
laying on them a single prohibition, for which, when they
disobey it, as they inevitably will, they will blame him.
("Ingrate"!) They had within them the ability to resist temptation: "I made them / Sufficient to have stood, though free to
fall" (III.99). If they fell, it's their own fault—and, by the way,
just because their Creator knows what they are going to do,
that doesn't get them off the hook either:

> they themselves decreed
> Their own revolt, not I: if I foreknew,
> Foreknowledge had no influence on their fault,
> Which had no less proved certain unforeknown.
> (III.116–19)

But God's Son steps forward and volunteers to remedy
this misery, to sacrifice himself for those who deserve no

redemption. Here the music should call back to that which accompanied Satan's acceptance of the role of Tempter—but now in a major, not a minor, key.

## Second Movement (*Allegro*)

After a brief introduction, in which Satan wrestles not so much with remorse as with regret, the first theme here is a terrestrial one: we see with a panoramic majesty this newly made world and its inhabitants. We see "hill and dale and plain" (IV.243), fruit-bearing trees, flowers, a natural fountain giving forth four streams, even flocks of sheep "Grazing the tender herb" (IV.253)—a new Creation so lovely that its very air is "able to drive / All sadness but despair" (IV.155f). And that very comment reminds us that we are seeing it all *through the eyes of Satan*: we perceive what he perceives, and when Milton reminds us that none of this is made for him, nor are their excellences fully accessible to his sensibilities—bent as he is on destruction—we should be reminded that in this sense we are more like Satan than like Adam and Eve. We are strangers here ourselves, we don't belong, and when Satan gets his first glimpse of Adam and Eve—

> Two of far nobler shape erect and tall,
> Godlike erect, with native honour clad
> In naked majesty seemed lords of all,
> And worthy seemed, for in their looks divine
> The image of their glorious maker shone. (IV.288–92)

—we might well make the same exclamation that Milton, in another witty turn, gives to Satan: "Oh hell!" (IV.358). But perhaps we may console ourselves by the thought that while Satan comes to destroy this shimmering world, we are merely the heirs of that destruction, participating in it, but not its initiators.

But how did it all come to this? To answer this question for Adam and Eve, God the Father sends the archangel Raphael to explain how Satan and his fellow rebels fell, that is, to narrate the War in Heaven. So begins the second theme (*Allegro agitato*) of this movement. Echoes of the earlier heavenly theme may perhaps be heard here, but they will quickly be overrun by a fiercer martial music. As I see it, Raphael's primary purpose is to establish the actual conditions under which the battle took place, which requires an anticipatory refutation of something that he knows Satan will tell Adam and Eve: that God is not God. In one key passage in Book V, Satan, responding to a discourse by the angel Abdiel about the Father and the Son, expresses skepticism:

> Doctrine which we would know whence learned:
>      who saw
> When this creation was? rememb'rest thou
> Thy making, while the maker gave thee being?
> We know no time when we were not as now;
> Know none before us, self-begot, self-raised
> By our own quickening power, when fatal course
> Had circled his full orb, the birth mature
> Of this our native heaven, ethereal sons. (V.856–63)

Satan's claim is that God—or "God"—did not make any of the angels; they made themselves when "fatal course" (some form of abstract destiny) decreed that the time was right. This above all Raphael determines to refute, and he does so by explaining that the War in Heaven was not between God and Satan—as the Manichaeans might have seen it, an eternal principle of Light and an eternal principle of Darkness—but rather between an army of righteous and obedient angels, led by Michael, and an army of arrogant and rebellious angels, led by Lucifer, later to be called Satan. Raphael expects that Satan will tell a very different story about what Obedience is from the true one, which is that it is the first necessity of Edenic life and wishes to forearm Adam and Eve against the lie's charms. He then goes on to tell Adam the story of his own creation, and that of the world, and answers many cosmological questions while declining to answer others.

## Third Movement (*Largo maestoso*)

"I now must change / Those notes to tragic" (IX.5–6), Milton tells us. Raphael's warning does no good, and Adam and Eve will enter our world, the broken world, the world of pain and death. This perhaps makes things easier for Milton, because to all of us who suffer and struggle and do things we know to be wrong, an unfallen and undivided state must remain mysterious, and this was as true for Milton as for any of us. Back in Book IV, when explaining to Eve the terms and conditions of the residence in Eden, he speaks of a God who requires

> From us no other service than to keep
> This one, this easy charge, of all the trees
> In Paradise that bear delicious fruit

So various, not to taste that only tree
Of knowledge, planted by the tree of life,
So near grows death to life, what e'er death is,
Some dreadful thing no doubt . . . (IV.420–26)

But how does he know what a "dreadful thing" is—he who has
never dreaded, never needed to dread, any creature or event?
This is but one example of the impossibility of describing a
world in which no evil has occurred—still more of describing
a *human consciousness* formed in such a world. To change one's
notes to tragic is to enter familiar ground.

But the particular form this tragedy takes can only be described by returning to the life of the poet, because one cannot
tell this story without articulating some account of the sexual
politics of Milton's Eden and how they relate to Milton's own
history with women.

Katherine Milton and her daughter died in 1658. The death
of his first wife, Mary, had prompted no public comment from
the poet, but Katherine's death seems to have crushed him, if
his poem "Methought I saw my late espoused saint" is to be
trusted. In his dream she

Came vested all in white, pure as her mind;
    Her face was veil'd, yet to my fancied sight
    Love, sweetness, goodness, in her person shin'd
So clear as in no face with more delight.
    But Oh! as to embrace me she inclin'd,
    I wak'd, she fled, and day brought back my night.

A double grief: in his dream he saw *her*, and in his dream he,
a blind man, *saw*.

In 1663, when Milton was working on *Paradise Lost* and (probably) *De Doctrina Christiana*, he married for the third time: the poet, then age fifty-four, wedded twenty-four-year-year-old Elizabeth Minshull. From all that we can tell—including the testimony of Elizabeth, who outlived her husband by fifty-three years and on several occasions spoke of him to inquirers—the marriage was a happy one; but the same cannot be said of Milton's relationship with his daughters from his first marriage, Anne, Mary, and Deborah, who at the time of his marriage to Elizabeth were ages sixteen, fourteen, and ten. Almost everything we know about his relationship with them is through second- and thirdhand testimony, most of it coming years after his death; which is to say that we *know* very little. But, for what it is worth, those testimonies have a certain troubling consistency.

Anne was disabled, partially lame and unable to speak clearly. The former disability might not have bothered Milton much, but he probably regretted the speech impediment, whatever it was, because after he became blind he relied on his daughters to read to him. Anne appears never to have learned to write, though Mary could at least sign her name, and Deborah must have been competently literate because later in life she ran a small school. Some people even said that Milton employed her as an amanuensis when his regular secretaries where unavailable. (Milton could get very anxious when he had composed verse but had no one to dictate it to—he felt, he said, like a cow that needed to be milked.) They all could read English, and it seems that Milton had them read to him from texts in foreign languages that they could not understand but had been taught to pronounce. Deborah, the youngest,

who married and moved to Ireland in the year of her father's
death and long outlived the rest, could recite large chunks of
Homer and Euripides in Greek, Isaiah in Hebrew, and Ovid
in Latin—but claimed not to know the meaning of the words
that came out of her mouth. Her father, she said, believed that
"one tongue is enough for a woman."[14]

Milton's nephew Edward Phillips, who as a boy was Milton's
pupil, felt sorry for the daughters: "They were condemned to
the performance of reading, and exactly pronouncing of all the
languages of whatever book he should at one time or other
think fit to peruse . . . All which sorts of books to be confined
to read, without understanding one word, must needs to a trial
of patience, almost beyond endurance." In 1662, the year before Milton's remarriage, the daughters had had enough, and
began to take their revenge: because they felt that their father
was a miser as well as a taskmaster, they stole money from the
housekeeping budget and even sold some of his books. Apparently he didn't bother to inform them that he planned to re-
marry, so when word got to Mary, she declared that she didn't
consider that news, but if she heard that her father was dead,
"that would be something."[15]

This distressing family history, or gossip, became a standard
part of Milton lore. In his brief life of Milton, Samuel Johnson
writes that "His family consisted of women; and there appears
in his books something like a Turkish contempt of females, as
subordinate and inferior beings. That his own daughters might
not break the ranks, he suffered them to be depressed by a

14. See Lewalski, *The Life*, p. 407.
15. See Lewalski, *The Life*, pp. 407, 409.

mean and penurious education. He thought woman made only for obedience, and man only for rebellion."[16] This has become something like the standard view of Milton, pursued most fiercely and at greatest length by Robert Graves in his novel *Wife to Mr. Milton* (1943). But if it is correct—and this is why I have returned to biographical matters—what implications does this "Turkish contempt" have for his portrayal of Eve in *Paradise Lost*? This takes us back to my account of this third movement of the poem, but in a way that must register the heat of the debates on how even a mere *summation* of the poem may rightly be made.

In the most commonly held view, from Dr. Johnson to modern feminist writers like Sandra Gilbert and Susan Gubar, Milton is not simply a Christian thinker who happens to hold the standard sexist views of his time. Rather, throughout *Paradise Lost* he takes great pains to insist upon Eve's inferiority to Adam and her intrinsic dependence on him. Milton says, when introducing the first couple of humanity to us, that they

> worthy seemed, for in their looks divine
> The image of their glorious maker shone,
> Truth, wisdom, sanctitude severe and pure,
> Severe but in true filial freedom placed;
> Whence true authority in men; though both
> Not equal, as their sex not equal seemed;
> For contemplation he and valour formed,

16. Samuel Johnson, "Life of Milton," in *The Lives of the Poets*, vols. 21–23 of *The Works of Samuel Johnson*, ed. John Middendorf, The Yale Edition of the Works of Samuel Johnson (New Haven: Yale University Press, 2010), vol. 21, p. 171.

For softness she and sweet attractive grace,
He for God only, she for God in him. (IV.291–99)[17]

His theology of female subordination thus appears in the first ten lines of their description. And if we have not grasped the point, he reinforces it by having Eve narrate her first sight of Adam, who comes into her world as she looks into a pool and marvels at the beauty of what she does not yet know is her own image. Nothing wrong with that, in the strict sense; after all, she is indeed beautiful, and does not have enough experience in the world to know that she's looking at herself. But it is a curious scene for Milton to have invented, especially with the emphatic echoes of the Narcissus story. And he has a very clear purpose behind it, because he goes on to have Eve tell us that when she saw Adam she found him attractive—but not nearly *as* attractive as the image in the pool, to which she immediately returned her attention. Adam has to *force* her away from self-contemplation and towards contemplation of him. "I yielded," she later declares, "and from that time see / How beauty is excelled by manly grace / And wisdom, which alone is truly fair" (IV.489–91).

It is noteworthy, according to this view, that when Milton first describes Eve he says that her hair was "Dishevelled, but in wanton ringlets waved" (IV.306)—*wanton*, a word that could in some circumstances mean merely abundant and

17. When the great classicist Richard Bentley decided that the text of *Paradise Lost*, like those of the ancient texts to which he gave most of his professional attention, was corrupt, he made his own edition (1732), in which he changed "she for God in him" to "she for God *and* him"; which, had Milton actually written it, would have done a lot to deliver him from the strongest accusations of misogyny.

luxurious, but of course it has a pejorative sense just waiting
to be activated. So, even in her unfallen state, perhaps *especially*
in her unfallen state, Eve is not capable of self-government;
she is made by God in such a way that she requires Adam to
set her on the proper path, because without him she will surely
take the wrong one. She has *not yet* taken the wrong one, but
wrong is inevitable to the mother of the human race unless she
is governed by her husband.

According to this account, one of the pivotal moments in
the story comes soon after Adam has been warned by the archangel Gabriel to be especially vigilant because a tempter has
come to their garden. Eve decides that she wants to go out for
a walk by herself, and when Adam tells her that that might not
be such a great idea, she replies with some asperity:

> Offspring of heaven and earth, and all earth's lord,
> That such an enemy we have, who seeks
> Our ruin, both by thee informed I learn,
> And from the parting angel overheard
> As in a shady nook I stood behind,
> Just then returned at shut of evening flowers.
> But that thou shouldst my firmness therefore doubt
> To God or thee, because we have a foe
> May tempt it, I expected not to hear.
> His violence thou fear'st not, being such,
> As we, not capable of death or pain,
> Can either not receive, or can repel.
> His fraud is then thy fear, which plain infers
> Thy equal fear that my firm faith and love
> Can by his fraud be shaken or seduced;

Thoughts, which how found they harbour in thy breast
Adam, misthought of her to thee so dear? (IX.273–89)

She's doubly offended, first that Adam would tell her something she already knows, second that he would doubt her ability to cope with temptation on her own. When he insists upon
the seriousness of Gabriel's charge, she replies,

If this be our condition, thus to dwell
In narrow circuit straitened by a foe,
Subtle or violent, we not endued
Single with like defence, wherever met,
How are we happy, still in fear of harm? (IX.322–26)

Adam has a strong answer to this, but having given it, having
as it were won the argument, he waives the point: "But if thou
think, trial unsought may find / Us both securer than thus
warned thou seem'st, / Go" (IX.370–72). He knows this is
wrong, he knows that this is an unwise decision, he knows that
he is supposed to watch over her, he knows that she is not
formed in such a way that she can function properly on her own
recognizance, but he lets her do it anyway, because her feelings
are hurt—we might say her *pride* is hurt—at his reluctance to
trust her to solitary movement through Eden.

We've come here to one of the great difficulties that Milton
faces, perhaps his greatest difficulty, which is how to depict
unfallen creatures who are in the process of falling. When Eve
has her vanity wounded, and Adam allows an action he knows
to be unwise because he defers to that wounded vanity, how
are they not both *already fallen*? How is the work of undermin-
ing their perfect state not already accomplished? The problem

is more pronounced in the case of Adam than in that of Eve, for if Milton believes that Eve was created to be dependent and subservient, then that she unsupervised and undirected would go astray is unsurprising, even necessary. That Adam should yield to her preferences is harder to understand: the key phrase here being his "But if thou think"—because, as he perfectly well knows, it is not what *she* thinks that is supposed to decide matters but rather what *he* thinks. When Adam is telling his story to Raphael in Book VIII—*before* the Fall—he says that while he knows that in certain senses she is inferior to him,

> yet when I approach
> Her loveliness, so absolute she seems
> And in her self complete, so well to know
> Her own, that what she wills to do or say,
> Seems wisest, virtuousest, discreetest, best . . .

To which the archangel responds first of all not with words but "with contracted brow"—this was not what he expected or wanted to hear (VIII.540ff).

Just as in his first descriptions of the Paradisal couple Milton had emphasized Eve's natural proclivity to wantonness, so in Books VIII and IV he emphasizes the simple fact that Adam *ought to have known better* than to allow this to happen; and he places renewed emphasis on that point when, after Eve has succumbed to the serpent's temptation and eaten the fruit, she tries to convince Adam to do so also, and succeeds. Milton says that Eve ate the fruit because she was deceived—a deception Adam's permission enabled—and adds that Adam "scrupled not to eat / Against his better knowledge, not deceived, / But fondly overcome with female charm" (IV.998–1000).[18] And Adam's action, for Milton, is the truly decisive one, the one that consigns us all to misery and death, because if Adam had not eaten the fruit then, though Eve would have died, he would have lived. God would have provided a new mate for him, perhaps by taking a rib from his other side; and indeed Eve's decision to try to persuade Adam to eat the fruit along with her is driven by her fear that this is indeed what will happen, that a second Eve will replace her—such an outcome is, for her, "a death to think" (IX.830). On the one hand, she would like to be the only one who eats the fruit so that she would be wiser than Adam, thus turning the tables; but, what if the story the serpent told her is wrong? What if she *isn't* wiser than Adam? What if what God says is true and she will die? In the end her fear overwhelms her desire for power and so she encourages him to eat. Which he does, thus, in Milton's view, sealing the fate of every human being who would ever live: through this one man's sin, as the apostle Paul would later write, all of us die (I Corinthians 15:22).

On the account I have been giving, the careful reader of this poem cannot doubt that Adam bears the greater responsibility, indeed in a sense the whole responsibility, for all of the

---

18. In early modern English "fond" often meant "foolish," as when King Lear says, "I am a very foolish fond old man" (IV.7). The biblical source for the idea that Adam was "not deceived" is I Timothy 2:17: "And Adam was not deceived, but the woman being deceived was in the transgression." But though Milton always claimed to take his ideas straight from Scripture, he surely knew that Augustine devotes some considerable time to this very point in his *City of God* (XIV.11), and the Augustinian development of the idea seems to have been influential in Milton's portrayal.

human misery that has come since he ate that fruit and that will come in the future. But this is no answer to those who refuse Milton's sexual politics and sexual theology; Adam is only responsible in this way because of his profound superiority to Eve, his possession of a sovereign reason which makes him superior to her not merely in degree but in kind. He is a wholly different creature from what she is; he is made for intimate relationship with God, and equal conversation with angels, and free action independent of any other created being; she is made for none of these things.

It would be difficult to argue that this account of Eve-in-relation-to-Adam is wholly wrong. Many elements of it are intrinsic not only to Milton's understanding of the story but also to the biblical story itself. But the account is incomplete; and, as is so often the case, *Paradise Lost* here proves resistant to straightforward interpretation—as does Milton himself. For instance, were Milton as profoundly misogynistic as he is often said to be, it is difficult to account for the section of his *Defensio Segunda* (*Second Defense of the English People*, 1654) devoted to the most extravagant praise of Queen Christina of Sweden: "With what honor, with what respect, O queen, ought I always to cherish you, whose exalted virtue and magnanimity are a source not alone of glory to you, but also of favor and benefit to me! They have freed me from all suspicion and ill-repute in the minds of other kings and by this glorious and immortal kindness have bound me to you for ever. How well ought foreigners to think of your fairness and justice!"[19]

19. PR 343. The encomium goes on for several hundred more words. Ruth Mohl, who in 1953 edited Milton's commonplace book in the *Complete Prose Works*

We might also be surprised by the perfect independence of
virtue that enables the Lady to resist the tempter Comus.

Moreover, when we look more closely at the character of
Eve as Milton depicts her we see something other than mere
subjugation. When Adam in Book VIII narrates his own history to Raphael, he describes the sense of incompleteness he
felt after the animals, "two and two" (VIII.350), approached
him to be named:

> Among unequals what society
> Can sort, what harmony or true delight?
> Which must be mutual, in proportion due
> Given and received; but in disparity
> The one intense, the other still remiss
> Cannot well suit with either, but soon prove
> Tedious alike: of fellowship I speak
> Such as I seek, fit to participate
> All rational delight, wherein the brute
> Cannot be human consort . . . (VIII.383–92)

And it is on precisely these grounds—the desire for *equal, mutual,* and *rational* fellowship—that God grants Adam's request.
A little later in the same discourse, he recalls that when he first
saw Eve, "on she came, Led by her heavenly maker, though
unseen, / And guided by his voice, nor uninformed / Of nup-
tial sanctity and marriage rites" (VIII.484–87)—thus making

---

of John Milton, vol. 1, *1624–1642* (New Haven: Yale University Press, 1953), com-
mented that the frequent praise of virtuous and otherwise gifted women in that
commonplace book calls into question "Milton's proverbial disesteem for women"
(p. 357).

it quite explicit that God speaks to Eve directly, not mediately
through her husband. Scenes like this do not cause the standard view to disappear, but they complicate it, as we will see
later in this chapter and occasionally throughout the book. As
Catherine Gimelli Martin has noted, the idea that Milton
manifested a "Turkish contempt of females" "would no doubt
have astonished both the poet himself and his contemporaries, the most critical of whom regarded his views on women
and marriage as libertine, not retrograde."[20]

But I now must change these notes to tragic. Having jointly
succumbed to the allure, not of the fruit, but of disobedience,
and having thus lost their self-governance, they fall into passionate embrace. Adam suddenly finds Eve "fairer now /
Than ever" (X.1032–33), something much appreciated by Eve,
"whose eye darted contagious fire" (X.1036). As we have seen,
this is not the first time they have sexual intercourse: that had
been part of their unfallen experience, as Milton makes explicit in a passage that "Whatever hypocrites austerely talk /
Of purity and place and innocence."[21] But now it's different,

20. Catherine Gimelli Martin, "Introduction" to *Milton and Gender* (Cambridge: Cambridge University Press, 2005), p. 1. For further explorations of these
vital matters, see the essays in that collection, and also Diane Kelsey McColley's
*Milton's Eve* (Urbana: University of Illinois Press, 1983) and Joseph Wittreich's
*Feminist Milton* (Ithaca: Cornell University Press, 1987). At the risk of becoming
too technical, I would suggest a distinction between *ontology* and *economy*. Onto-
logically, Adam and Eve are equal; but in the "home economics" of Eden, Eve is
right to address Adam as "My author and disposer" (IV.635).

21. IV.744–45. The physical intimacy of Adam and Eve is one of the things that
most agonizes Satan, who acts as a demonic Peeping Tom in this scene:

    Sight hateful, sight tormenting! thus these two
    Emparadised in one another's arms
    The happier Eden, shall enjoy their fill

and I have tried to indicate the nature of the difference by using the word *passionate*—from the Latin *passio*, meaning, among other things, to suffer. Before they chose sexual intimacy; now sexuality chooses them, they undergo it, they suffer it. Having sought to claim autonomy, they find themselves overmastered by their own desire.

## Fourth Movement (*Andante*)

The final movement, like the first and second, features two contrasting themes—two consequences of the great tragedy that unfolded in the third movement. The first of those themes, the conclusion of Satan's story, contains one of Milton's wittiest musical moments. Satan returns to give an account of his achievement, a tale he relates with relish, and concludes with an invitation: "Ye have the account / Of my performance: what remains, ye gods, / But up and enter now into full bliss" (X.501–3). But the sibilance of that finally syllable receives a mocking echo:

> So having said, a while he stood, expecting
> Their universal shout and high applause
> To fill his ear, when contrary he hears
> On all sides, from innumerable tongues
> A dismal universal hiss, the sound
> Of public scorn . . .

---

Of bliss on bliss, while I to hell am thrust,
Where neither joy nor love, but fierce desire,
Among our other torments not the least,
Still unfulfilled with pain of longing pines! (IV.505–11)

For he is at that moment transformed into a serpent—
"punished in the shape he sinned, / According to his doom"—
while his infernal soldiery are made into "complicated
monsters," so that "dreadful was the din / Of hissing through
the hall"—hissing, but no longer any speech. The word *monster*
is from the Latin *monstrum*, a showing, a revelation, and also
a warning (from *monere*, to warn). The consequences of their
sin are now *demonstrated* in their bodies and voices, forever.

The second theme takes us back to Eden—paradisal music,
though now in a minor key; still lovely, but sobered. Adam
and Eve have fallen into guilt, shame, regret—and mutual recrimination, as we're told in the final words of Book IX: "Thus
they in mutual accusation spent / The fruitless hours, but neither self-condemning, / And of their vain contest appeared no
end." Is there no hope for them?

The situation is unpromising. When confronted by God,
Adam pompously announces his reluctance "to accuse / My
other self, the partner of my life" (X.127–28), but accuse her he
does, and even suggests a certain lack of foresight on God's part:
"This woman whom thou mad'st to be my help, / And gav'st me
as thy perfect gift"—This is your idea, my Lord, of a perfect
gift?—"so good, / So fit, so acceptable, so divine, / That from her
hand I could suspect no ill"—being afflicted by this *supposedly*
fit and acceptable and divine companion, and being deceived by
her, what did you expect?—"I did eat" (X.124–43).

The contrast between Adam and Eve is here especially
noteworthy: When asked what she did, she replies, "The
serpent me beguiled and I did eat" (X.162). If this sounds also
like self-justification, note that it is precisely what happened.
And Eve does not elaborate by blaming Adam for not protect-

ing her, or God for having assigned her so inept and neglectful a companion. She simply confesses, in eight simple words.

As the tenth book moves on, the contrast strengthens: Adam embarks on a lengthy soliloquy—from line 720 to line 844—in which he resumes his blaming of God ("Wherefore didst thou beget me? I sought it not") and, somewhat comically, of Eve: "that bad woman." When he sees Eve, who sits silent and "desolate where she sat" (864), he turns his wrath directly on her: "Out of my sight, thou serpent" (867): "but for thee / I had persisted happy" (873–74).

To this scornful loathing, Eve's response, one of the most heartbreakingly gorgeous passages in all of poetry, begins with a simple plea: "Forsake me not thus, Adam" (914). C. S. Lewis has pointed out that before the Fall Adam and Eve "hardly ever address each other simply by their names, but by stately periphrases; *Fair Consort, My Author and Disposer, Daughter of God and Man, accomplisht Eve, O Sole in whom my thoughts find all repose.*"[22] And this is true, but while Lewis thinks the change a result of their being "robbed of their original majesty," I think Eve's calling of Adam by his name marks the only thought, at this desperate moment, of a lover who fears the loss of her beloved. "Forsake me not thus, Adam."

As Eve continues, she blames neither Adam nor God: she blames only herself, and seeks only reconciliation with her beloved:

While yet we live, scarce one short hour perhaps,
Between us two let there be peace, both joining,

22. Lewis, *A Preface to "Paradise Lost,"* pp. 119–20.

As joined in injuries, one enmity
Against a foe by doom express assigned us,
That cruel serpent: on me exercise not
Thy hatred for this misery befallen,
On me already lost, me than thyself
More miserable; both have sinned, but thou
Against God only, I against God and thee,
And to the place of judgment will return,
There with my cries importune heaven, that all
The sentence from thy head removed may light
On me, sole cause to thee of all this woe,
Me me only just object of his ire. (X.923–36)

And so *grace* enters human history; grace to the graceless, forgiveness to the unforgiving; the first turning of the other cheek; an urgent generosity whose urgency is powerfully conveyed in those three unpunctuated words: *Me me only*.[23] Eve will pay

---

23. Just a few moments earlier, Adam had said almost the same thing:

> . . . all my evasions vain,
> And reasonings, though through mazes, lead me still
> But to my own conviction: first and last
> On me, me only, as the source and spring
> Of all corruption, all the blame lights due;
> So might the wrath. Fond wish! couldst thou support
> That burden heavier than the earth to bear,
> Than all the world much heavier, though divided
> With that bad woman? (X.829–37)

But we see here how quickly his recognition of his own corruption gives way to condemnation of "that bad woman"—and then, immediately after this, he forgets his own role and denounces her as "that serpent." What in Adam is only a passing mood of self-reproach is in the "desolate" Eve a settled conviction.

whatever price so that she and her husband may be reconciled while they yet live—for she knows that "of the tree of the knowledge of good and evil . . . in the day that thou eatest thereof thou shalt surely die" (Gen. 2:17). Adam reciprocates this urge to reconciliation, but the key point here is that he can *only* reciprocate: grace begins not in him, but in the desolate heart of Eve.

Thus it is with Eve's initial offering of grace that the history of redemption begins. It is only after this essential moment that another archangel—this time Michael, the warrior who led the armies of the Lord against Satan and his fellow rebels and cast them down into Hell—comes to this breaking Eden to tell them that much hope remains, because God has chosen to redeem fallen humanity. Michael's account of future history, his tale of "the race of time" (XII.554), is a narrative-poetic tactic cribbed straight from the sixth book of Virgil's *Aeneid*, in which Aeneas's father, Anchises, hoping to encourage his son's strength of will, narrates the glories-to-come of imperial Rome; it is also a vital part of Milton's overall strategy of declaring *his* epic to be grander than those of his predecessors.[24] However essential Michael's story to Milton's epic architecture, it has not found widespread admiration: C. S. Lewis, in a famous passage from his book on the poem,

---

24. At the outset of Book IX Milton had declared his self-chosen responsibility:

> sad task, yet argument
> Not less but more heroic than the wrath
> Of stern Achilles on his foe pursued
> Thrice fugitive about Troy wall; or rage
> Of Turnus for Lavinia disespoused,
> Or Neptune's ire or Juno's . . .

has written that Milton was "not content with following his master in the use of occasional prophecies, allusions, and reflections," but instead makes his two last books into a brief outline of sacred history from the Fall to the Last Day. "Such an untransmuted lump of futurity, coming in a position so momentous for the structural effect of the whole work, is inartistic."[25] The phrase *untransmuted lump of futurity* is a singularly apt one, widely quoted by scholars; if Milton, wherever he may be, knows it, I am sure that it brings a blush to his spectral cheek. And to have something so "inartistic" appear quite near the conclusion of a majestic work of literary art—this is deeply regrettable.

However, as Lewis also says, there is "a great recovery at the very end." Having completed his story of the "great deliverance" to come, Michael encourages Adam to relate it to Eve (whom Michael has cast into a sleep eased by good dreams) so that they will be "Both in one faith unanimous though sad, / With cause for evils past, yet much more cheered / With meditation on the happy end" (XII.602–4). Adam for his part responds to Michael's good news with a soaring aria of joyful gratitude:

> O goodness infinite, goodness immense!
> That all this good of evil shall produce,
> And evil turn to good; more wonderful
> Than that which by creation first brought forth
> Light out of darkness! full of doubt I stand,
> Whether I should repent me now of sin
> By me done and occasioned, or rejoice

25. Lewis, *A Preface to "Paradise Lost,"* p. 129.

Much more, that much more good thereof shall spring,
To God more glory, more good will to men
From God, and over wrath grace shall abound.
   (XII.469–78)

Those concluding lines obviously echo the angelic message given to "shepherds abiding in the field, keeping watch over their flock by night": they hear the announcement of the birth of the Messiah, and then "suddenly there was with the angel a multitude of the heavenly host praising God, and saying, Glory to God in the highest, and on earth peace, good will toward men" (Luke 2:8–14).

———

What remains is only a quiet dismissal: strings playing *piano* as the Father and Mother of all humanity depart the garden which, to this point, is all they know:

Some natural tears they dropped, but wiped them
   soon;
The world was all before them, where to choose
Their place of rest, and providence their guide:
They hand in hand with wandering steps and slow,
Through Eden took their solitary way.

# 3

# Changing Fortunes

*PARADISE LOST* appeared in 1667. If the poem sold poorly at first, that was largely the result of Milton's having chosen the wrong bookseller—which is to say, the wrong publisher. In the seventeenth century, the modern system of book publication and distribution had not yet been developed: often enough, a book would be printed in the back room of a shop and sold from the front room. In 1674 Milton made some changes. While the poem had originally been published in ten books, he reorganized it into twelve books, to match the *Aeneid*. (Why he didn't do that to start with has always been a mystery.) Then, in response to complaints about the difficulty of his poem, he provided "Arguments," that is, summaries, for each book.[1] It has long been customary to prepend each

1. Here, as an example, is the Argument of Book IV:

   Satan now in prospect of Eden, and nigh the place where he must now attempt the bold enterprise which he undertook alone against God and man, falls into many doubts with himself, and many passions, fear, envy, and despair; but at length confirms himself in evil, journeys on to Paradise, whose outward prospect and situation is described, overleaps the bounds, sits in

In the year of Our Lord Christ
One thousand seven hundred thirty and seven
This Bust
of the Author of PARADISE LOST
was placed here by William Benson Esquire
One of the two Auditors of the Imprests
to his Majesty King George the second
formerly
Surveyor General of the Works
to his Majesty King George the first
Rysbrack
was the Statuary who cut it.

FIGURE 3. Monument to Milton, featuring a bust
by John Michael Rysbrack, in Westminster Abbey; installed in 1737.
Photo: 14GTR. CC BY-SA 4.0.

Argument to its book, but initially they were all placed at the beginning of the volume, presumably to give bookshop browsers a sense of how the whole story would come out before they committed to a purchase.

Though these changes did lead to improved sales, at first there were many readers who might have been interested in the topic but would never have read a book by a "Regicide." This was how Milton was known in those years: as a political figure, one who had celebrated the beheading of King Charles I and who had worked in the government of the man, Oliver Cromwell, who had made that beheading happen. It was impossible in those days to disentangle Milton's reputation as a poet, such as it was, from his reputation as a political figure,

---

the shape of a cormorant on the tree of life, as highest in the garden to look about him. The garden described; Satan's first sight of Adam and Eve; his wonder at their excellent form and happy state, but with resolution to work their fall; overhears their discourse, thence gathers that the tree of knowledge was forbidden them to eat of, under penalty of death; and thereon intends to found his temptation, by seducing them to transgress: then leaves them awhile, to know further of their state by some other means. Meanwhile Uriel descending on a sunbeam warns Gabriel, who had in charge the gate of Paradise, that some evil spirit had escaped the deep, and passed at noon by his sphere in the shape of a good angel down to Paradise, discovered after by his furious gestures in the mount. Gabriel promises to find him ere morning. Night coming on, Adam and Eve discourse of going to their rest: their bower described; their evening worship. Gabriel drawing forth his bands of night-watch to walk the round of Paradise, appoints two strong angels to Adam's bower, lest the evil spirit should be there doing some harm to Adam or Eve sleeping; there they find him at the ear of Eve, tempting her in a dream, and bring him, though unwilling, to Gabriel; by whom questioned, he scornfully answers, prepares resistance, but hindered by a sign from heaven, flies out of Paradise.

and even into the nineteenth century people's opinions about Milton were often shaped by their views of the Civil War and Cromwell's Protectorate.

A fair representation of the Royalist view of Milton appears in Sir Walter Scott's novel about the English Civil War, *Woodstock* (1826), of which the Cavalier Sir Henry Lee is the protagonist. In response to Sir Henry's expressed doubt that the Cromwellian movement, populated as it is by "saints and prophets without end," would be likely to produce any worthwhile poets, his nephew Colonel Everard declares, "I know verses written by a friend of the Commonwealth, and those, too, of a dramatic character, which, weighed in an impartial scale, might equal even the poetry of Shakspeare." He then recites a passage from Milton's masque *Comus*. When he finally reveals their author, this is what happens:

> "John Milton!" exclaimed Sir Henry in astonishment. "What! John Milton, the blasphemous and bloody-minded author of the *Defensio Populi Anglicani*!—the advocate of the infernal High Court of Fiends!—the creature and parasite of that grand impostor, that loathsome hypocrite, that detestable monster, that prodigy of the universe, that disgrace of mankind, that landscape of iniquity, that sink of sin, and that compendium of baseness, Oliver Cromwell!"[2]

By the "High Court of Fiends" Sir Henry refers not to Satan and his followers in Pandemonium but rather to Cromwell's system of tracking and persecuting royalists. That a "creature and parasite of that grand imposter" could be a poet *at all* is

2. Sir Walter Scott, *Woodstock*, Chapter XXV.

inconceivable to Sir Henry. For him and for many royalists, during the Protectorate and Restoration alike, Milton is no more or less or other than a political revolutionary.

His fellow poets thought otherwise. When John Dryden began work with Milton at Cromwell's government, in 1657, he was twenty-six and just starting his poetic career. One of his first significant poems was his "Heroic Stanzas on the Death of Oliver Cromwell" (1659), written under the expectation that the Protectorate would continue for some time. When, the following year, the monarchy was restored, Dryden immediately wrote "*Astraea Redux*: A Poem on the Happy Restoration and Return of His Second Majesty Charles II"— as complete and adroit a reversal as one can readily imagine. An ongoing series of poems flattering the Stuart regime led, ultimately, to Dryden's being appointed Poet Laureate in 1668. At this point people remembered his poem in praise of Cromwell—"His name a great example stands to show / How strangely high endeavours may be blessed / Where piety and valour jointly go"[3]—which led to some embarrassment, perhaps, but not to an apology.

When the capacious Theatre Royal opened in London in 1674, Dryden saw an opportunity to create something spectacular: *The State of Innocence: An Opera*, he called it—a dramatic adaptation of *Paradise Lost* in heroic couplets. Milton's decision to write in blank verse (unrhymed iambic pentameter) had been much scorned when his poem appeared, and in 1668, for the fourth printing of the first edition—the poem

3. *John Dryden* (Oxford Authors), ed. Keith Walker (Oxford: Oxford University Press, 1987), pp. 1, 6, 9.

evidently had not been *wholly* unsuccessful—he added an ir-
ritable note insisting that rhyme is "no necessary adjunct or
true ornament" but rather "the invention of a barbarous age."
After all, neither Homer nor Virgil used rhyme; with their example in mind he cast himself as a kind of liberator: though
"vulgar readers" may think the poem's rhymelessness a defect,
it is rather "an example set . . . of ancient liberty recovered to
heroic poem from the troublesome and modern bondage of
rhyming" (PL 55). In light of this lofty insistence, Dryden's decision to retell the story in rhymed couplets might have been
deemed a criticism. So Dryden visited the old blind poet—
now in the last months of his life—and asked permission to
adapt the epic for the stage, which Milton granted. What he
thought about Dryden's project has not been recorded.

Earlier we noted the passage in which Milton emphasizes
that Satan would never have been able to lift his head from the
floor of Hell had God not expressly permitted it. Immediately
after that aside, Satan speaks:

> "Is this the region, this the soil, the clime,"
> Said then the lost Archangel, "this the seat
> That we must change for Heaven?—this mournful
>     gloom
> For that celestial light? Be it so, since He
> Who now is sovran can dispose and bid
> What shall be right. . . ."

Here's how Dryden rewrites it:

> Is this the Seat our Conqueror has given?
> And this the Climate we must change for Heaven?

These Regions and this Realm my Wars have got;
This Mournful Empire is the Loser's Lot:
In Liquid Burnings or on Dry to dwell,
Is all the sad Variety of Hell.

In the end, Dryden was not able to get his "opera" staged—the requisite stagecraft was deemed too expensive—but he published *The State of Innocence* as a book, and for the next few decades it significantly outsold *Paradise Lost*.

Whether his adaptation is essentially an homage or essentially a criticism is hard to say. Dryden's shifty political trimming makes it difficult to know what he really thought about almost anything. At times he expressed significant doubts about Milton's project: its "subject is not that of an heroic poem, properly so called," because "His design is the losing of our happiness; his event is not prosperous, like that of all other epic works; his heavenly machines are many, and his human persons are but two."[4] (It is hard to see what is "prosperous" about the story of the *Iliad*, but for Dryden, like most poets of his age, including Milton himself, Virgil looms larger than Homer.) By "machines" here Dryden seems to be thinking of almost all the figures in the poem: angels, demons, Sin, Death—perhaps even God himself—figures who occupy fixed places in the development of the story and are therefore machine-like in their effects. In another comment Dryden wittily pretends that Milton wrote the very tale of "gorgeous Knights / At Joust and Tournament" that he rejected: Milton's

4. John Dryden, "A Discourse Concerning the Original and Progress of Satire" (1693), in *Of Dramatic Poesy and Other Critical Essays*, ed. George Watson (London: Dent, Everyman's Library, 1962), vol. 2, p. 84.

poem would have been more truly epic "if the Devil had not been his hero, instead of Adam; if the giant had not foiled the knight, and driven him out of his stronghold, to wander through the world with his lady errant; and if there had not been more machining persons than human in his poem."[5] Notice here the first appearance of an idea we will see much of: that Satan is the real hero of Milton's poem.

Yet Dryden would also write this "epigram" for an edition of *Paradise Lost*:

Three Poets, in three distant Ages born,
Greece, Italy, and England did adorn.
The First in loftiness of thought surpassed;
The Next in Majesty; in both the Last.
The force of Nature could no farther go:
To make a third she joined the former two.

It is difficult to imagine higher praise than to describe a poet as Homer and Virgil combined. And yet it's worth noting that these lines were published in 1688, as the Stuart regime Dryden had so vigorously supported was on its way out, to be replaced by those sound Protestants William and Mary. Perhaps the time was ripe for rehabilitating the old revolutionary?

Perhaps; but political shrewdness was not Dryden's forte. Demonstrating the same lack of foresight that he had exhibited when praising Cromwell in 1659, Dryden had converted to Catholicism in 1685, immediately upon the accession of the

5. Dryden's dedication of his translation of the *Aeneid*, "To the Most Honourable John, Lord Marquess of Normanby," in *Of Dramatic Poesy and Other Critical Essays*, vol. 2, p. 233.

Catholic James II to the throne—and then followed that up with
a pro-Catholic, anti-Anglican allegorical poem, *The Hind and the
Panther*, published when James had but a year remaining on
the throne. It is hard to give Dryden credit for *shrewd* calculation;
it is more likely that he really did think so highly of Milton.

In any event, while Dryden was clearly fascinated by, even
obsessed with, Milton—Miltonic echoes fill his poetry—his
explicit public comments are few and brief. The elevation of
Milton to a permanent position in the literary pantheon, and
of *Paradise Lost* to the status of transcendent classic, was largely
the work of a writer of the next generation: Joseph Addison.

Addison is a remarkable figure, too little noticed these days.
Though he lived only forty-seven years, he made quite a name
for himself as poet, dramatist, controversialist, and politician.
He was an early protégé of Dryden's, later a friend (and then
enemy) of Alexander Pope; a mover and shaker in politics and
literary culture alike; and, most important for our purposes
here, the co-creator, with his friend (and then enemy) Richard
Steele of that great literary genre the periodical essay. The first
of these periodicals, the *Tatler*, was dominated by Steele, but in
the second and more important, the *Spectator*, Steele and Addison shared the work. Between March 1711 and December 1712
the *Spectator* appeared six days a week (!), with Addison and
Steele writing most of the copy—an astonishing 250 essays
each. And once a week from January to May 1712, Addison
published essays on *Paradise Lost*—eighteen in all, enough to
make a short book.[6] And if we take the essays *as* a book, they

6. The *Spectator* essays are numbered, and Addison's essays on *Paradise Lost*,
which he published on Saturdays, are numbers 267, 273, 279, 285, 291, 297, 303, 309,

constitute the most important one ever written about Milton's poem, for they set the terms for much future debate.

This was, it should be said, not the first time Addison had written about Milton. In 1694, when he was twenty-two and pursuing his Master of Arts degree at Oxford, he wrote "An Account of the Greatest English Poets," in which he celebrated Chaucer, Spenser, Abraham Cowley—largely forgotten now, but then famous for his biblical epic *Davideis*—and Milton, of whom he says,

> Whate'er his pen describes I more than see,
> Whilst ev'ry verse, array'd in majesty,
> Bold, and sublime, my whole attention draws,
> And seems above the critics' nicer laws.

But he concludes his account of Milton thus:

> Oh had the poet ne'er profan'd his pen,
> To varnish o'er the guilt of faithless men;
> His other works might have deserv'd applause!
> But now the language can't support the cause,
> While the clean current, though serene and bright,
> Betrays a bottom odious to the sight.

*Paradise Lost*, then, deserves the highest praise; but "his other works" are defaced by his apologetics for Cromwellian tyranny.

Nearly twenty years later, when writing his *Spectator* essays, Addison felt that the years of civil war had receded sufficiently

---

315, 321, 327, 333, 339, 345, 351, 357, 363, and 369—the first appearing on 5 January and the last on 3 May 1712.

from memory—by 1712 most of those who remembered the conflict were dead—that he could celebrate Milton's great poem almost without reference to those "other works." Milton was thus well on his way to becoming a poet *simpliciter*, all thoughts of his revolutionary endeavors effectively banished.

I suspect that these essays were initially provoked by the critical comments of Dryden, Addison's quondam mentor. Addison is surely thinking of Dryden's claim that Milton's "subject is not that of an heroic poem, properly so called" when he writes in his first essay that "I shall waive the discussion of that point which was started some years since, whether Milton's *Paradise Lost* may be called an heroic poem" (no. 267). But he does not waive it for long, in part because he remembers another key claim by Dryden, that if Adam really is the heroic "knight" he is a knight defeated by a wicked "giant." In his fourth essay Addison writes:

> There is another objection against Milton's fable . . . namely, that the hero in the *Paradise Lost* is unsuccessful, and by no means a match for his enemies. This gave occasion to Mr. Dryden's reflection, that the devil was in reality Milton's hero. I think I have obviated this objection in my first paper. The *Paradise Lost* is an epic, or a narrative poem, and he that looks for a hero in it searches for that which Milton never intended; but if he will needs fix the name of an hero upon any person in it, it is certainly the Messiah who is the hero, both in the principal action and in the chief episodes. (no. 297)

Here Addison seems to be thinking that it is *tragedy* that must have a hero, not epic, and since Milton's poem is not a tragedy, it would be no fault in it if it lacked a hero. But, Addison says, you could quite plausibly say that the poem has a hero: Messiah, the Christ. The implicit argument here is that by associating *Paradise Lost* with chivalric tales, Dryden has missed the key *theological* axiom of the poem: that the essential conflict here is between the Enemy who seeks to destroy those humans made in the image of God and the Son (Messiah) who redeems them from the consequences of that demonic assault. Thus in Milton's poem Messiah is the protagonist, Satan the antagonist, and Adam and Eve the field of battle.

Whether this is an adequate account of the matter may be debated. Indeed, almost every statement one might make about *Paradise Lost*, even the most apparently anodyne, may be debated; it is, of all great poems, the most elusive of description—a claim that subsequent pages will amply bear out. Addison himself, in later essays, moves Adam and Eve more to the center of the story, and in the final essay says that "the principal fable"—"fable" is Addison's word for "plot" or "narrative"—of the poem "turns upon Adam and Eve" (no. 369). But he is consistent in his belief that Dryden has failed to understand the fully theological character of the poem.

Among the many points in his essays that will be raised again and elaborated by later readers and critics, three will be of particular importance.

*First*, Addison believes that Milton's portrayal in verse of the words and thoughts of God is inadequate to their subject: "If Milton's majesty forsakes him anywhere, it is in those parts of his poem where the Divine Persons are introduced as speakers. One may, I think, observe that the author proceeds with a kind of fear and trembling whilst he describes the sentiments of the

Almighty. He dares not give his imagination its full play, but chooses to confine himself to such thoughts as are drawn from the books of the most orthodox divines, and to such expressions as may be met with in Scripture. The beauties, therefore, which we are to look for in these speeches, are not of a poetical nature, nor so proper to fill the mind with sentiments of grandeur as with thoughts of devotion" (no. 315).

*Second,* he acknowledges that the poem is too difficult, and difficult because it betrays "an unnecessary ostentation of learning. . . . It is certain that both Homer and Virgil were masters of all the learning of their times, but it shows itself in their works after an indirect and concealed manner. Milton seems ambitious of letting us know, by his excursions on free-will and predestination, and his many glances upon history, astronomy, geography, and the like, as well as by the terms and phrases he sometimes makes use of, that he was acquainted with the whole circle of arts and sciences" (no. 297).

A feature of the poem that later readers would severely reprobate, Addison commends: the treatment of Adam and Eve in their unfallen state. I think he is again responding to Dryden—"his heavenly machines are many, and his human persons are but two"—when he writes,

> If we look into the characters of Milton we shall find that he has introduced all the variety his fable was capable of receiving. The whole species of mankind was in two persons at the time to which the subject of his poem is confined. We have, however, four distinct characters in these two persons. We see man and woman in the highest innocence and perfection, and in the most abject state of guilt and infirmity. The two last characters are, indeed, very common and

obvious; but the two first are not only more magnificent, but more new than any characters either in Virgil or Homer, or indeed in the whole circle of nature. (no. 273)

It is a brilliant comment, if not altogether convincing. If Milton indeed follows the biblical narrative on which he claims to base his "fable," two humans are all he had to choose from— and yet he contrives to double each of them, and to make them equally compelling in their innocent and fallen states.

When observing Milton's treatment of the Fall and its consequences, Addison is noticeably sympathetic to both persons. "Though Adam involves the whole species in misery, his crime proceeds from a weakness which every man is inclined to pardon and commiserate, as it seems rather the frailty of human nature than of the person who offended. Every one is apt to excuse a fault which he himself might have fallen into." But: "The part of Eve in this book is no less passionate and apt to sway the reader in her favor. She is represented with great tenderness as approaching Adam, but is spurned from him with a spirit of upbraiding and indignation conformable to the nature of man, whose passions had now gained the dominion over him" (no. 357).

This leads us to the *third* point that would occupy later readers: the question of whether Adam and Eve are characters with whom the ordinary reader can sympathetically engage— whether they are *relatable*, as today's readers might say, in a formulation that's not as anachronistic as it might seem.[7]

---

7. Edward Mendelson, in his superb book *The Things That Matter: What Seven Classic Novels Have to Say about the Stages of Life*: "Anyone, I think, who reads a novel for pleasure or instruction takes an interest both in the closed fictional world of that novel and in the ways the book provides models or examples of the kinds

Addison believes that we are intimately and necessarily connected to Adam and Eve—as we can see from his comment on "human nature" quoted above. What we call "human nature" is precisely what Adam and Eve brought into the world; we have all inherited it from them. He clinches the point thus:

> Milton's poem is admirable in this respect, since it is impossible for any of its readers, whatever nation, country, or people he may belong to, not to be related to the persons who are the principal actors in it; but what is still infinitely more to its advantage, the principal actors in this poem are not only our progenitors, but our representatives. We have an actual interest in everything they do, and no less than our utmost happiness is concerned and lies at stake in all their behavior. (no. 273)

Therefore the moral of the story—and Addison believes that "no just heroic poem ever was or can be made, from whence one great moral may not be deduced"—is "the most universal and most useful that can be imagined": "It is, in short, this, that obedience to the will of God makes men happy, and that disobedience makes them miserable." The permanent and absolute relevance of this moral makes *Paradise Lost*—whatever

---

of life that a reader might or might not choose to live. Most novels of the past two centuries that are still worth reading were written to respond to both these interests. They were not written to be read objectively or dispassionately, as if by some nonhuman intelligence, and they can be understood most fully if they are interpreted and understood from a personal point of view, not only from historical, thematic, or analytical perspectives. A reader who identifies with the characters in a novel is not reacting in a naïve way that ought to be outgrown or transcended, but is performing one of the central acts of literary understanding" (p. xii).

its poetic excellences, of which Addison believes there are a multitude—"more useful and instructive than any other poem in any language" (no. 369). Q.E.D.

Thanks largely to the praise of Dryden and Addison, a memorial to Milton was erected in Westminster Abbey in 1737. Some years earlier a Flemish sculptor resident in London named John Michael Rysbrack had made a bust of Milton; it was acquired by one William Benson, who made it the centerpiece of the monument, though that prominence is challenged by the long inscription below it. (Samuel Johnson would later say that "in our time a monument has been erected in Westminster-Abbey To the Author of Paradise Lost, by Mr. Benson, who has in the inscription bestowed more words upon himself than upon Milton."[8]) Whatever the motives or interests of Mr. Benson, the display of this monument in Westminster Abbey, near monuments to Chaucer and Spenser, suggests that the old regicide had finally been forgiven by the custodians of the very establishment he had worked to overthrow. And he got his place in Poets' Corner three years before Shakespeare was thus acknowledged.

———

We have moved along by generational hops: first Dryden (twenty-three years younger than Milton), then Addison (thirty-one years younger than Dryden), and now we turn to Samuel Johnson (thirty-seven years younger than Addison). If Addison establishes the terms on which later debates about

8. Samuel Johnson, "Life of Milton," p. 165.

the theology of *Paradise Lost* would be conducted, Johnson, in his brief "Life of Milton," offers a deeper engagement with the poem than any previously offered.

The biography is one of his great *Lives of the Most Eminent English Poets*, which he wrote late in his life, between 1779 and 1781. Because Johnson always wears his heart on his sleeve, we know that he would have preferred to leave Milton out of the series: "The Life of Milton has been already written in so many forms and with such minute enquiry that I might perhaps more properly have contented myself with the addition of a few notes to Mr. Fenton's elegant Abridgement, but that a new narrative was thought necessary to the uniformity of this edition."[9] (Elijah Fenton had in 1725 published an edition of Milton's *Complete Poetical Works*, prefaced with a very brief— five or six pages—biography of the poet. This Johnson viewed as completely adequate.)

Johnson did not like Milton. A sardonic tone pervades the biography. Of Milton's early poems he writes, "they would in any numerous school have obtained praise, but not excited wonder." Milton, after taking his Master of Arts, lived with his father in Buckinghamshire, "in which time he is said to have read all the Greek and Latin writers. With what limitations this universality is to be understood who shall inform us?" Once he becomes an author, "It appears in all his writings that he had the usual concomitant of great abilities, a lofty and steady confidence in himself, perhaps not without some contempt of others; for scarcely any man ever wrote so much and praised so few." Of Milton's years as a schoolmaster, at a period

9. Johnson, "Life of Milton," pp. 101–2.

when civil conflict was intensifying: "Let not our veneration for Milton forbid us to look with some degree of merriment on great promises and small performance, on the man who hastens home because his countrymen are contending for their liberty, and, when he reaches the scene of action, vapours away his patriotism in a private boarding-school. This is the period of his life from which all his biographers seem inclined to shrink." On the report that Milton's favorite among his poems was *Paradise Regained*: "Milton, however it happened, had this prejudice, and had it to himself."[10] And so on.

More deeply and seriously does Dr. Johnson suspect Milton's evident disdain for the Church of England: "Milton, who appears to have had full conviction of the truth of Christianity, and to have regarded the Holy Scriptures with the profoundest veneration, to have been untainted by any heretical peculiarity of opinion, and to have lived in a confirmed belief of the immediate and occasional agency of Providence, yet grew old without any visible worship." What is one to make of this neglect? Johnson issues what looks like a decisive negative verdict: "In the distribution of his hours, there was no hour of prayer, either solitary or with his household; omitting public prayers, he omitted all."[11]

None of this is really surprising, because Johnson was a committed Tory and Milton's republicanism, and still more his support of regicide, appalled him. His most definitive and complete judgment on Milton may be found in these sentences:

10. Johnson, "Life of Milton," pp. 104, 109–10, 112, 115–16, 163.
11. Johnson, "Life of Milton," p. 170.

Milton's republicanism was, I am afraid, founded in an envious hatred of greatness, and a sullen desire of independence; in petulance impatient of control, and pride disdainful of superiority. He hated monarchs in the state and prelates in the church; for he hated all whom he was required to obey. It is to be suspected that his predominant desire was to destroy rather than establish, and that he felt not so much the love of liberty as repugnance to authority.[12]

We can see then that Addison's attempts to set Milton's politics clearly apart from his poetry had not achieved complete success—but nor had they wholly failed. As Boswell noted in his *Life of Johnson*, "His just abhorrence of Milton's political notions was ever strong. But this did not prevent his warm admiration of Milton's great poetical merit, to which he has done illustrious justice, beyond all who have written upon the subject"[13]—because when Johnson turns to *Paradise Lost* his tone brightens considerably.

That may be putting it too mildly: Johnson writes straightforwardly that Milton's epic is "a poem which, considered with respect to design, may claim the first place, and with respect to performance the second, among the productions of the human mind."[14] But these are critical judgments about poetry *qua* poetry: an artful "design" and the execution in artful

12. Johnson, "Life of Milton," p. 171.

13. James Boswell, *Life of Johnson* (Oxford: Oxford University Press, 1953), p. 162. At several points in the *Life* Boswell pauses in his narrative to defend Johnson against the charge, which must have been a common one, that he was unjustly hostile to Milton.

14. Johnson, "Life of Milton," p. 182. Homer, then, is for Johnson Milton's only rival.

words of that design. Our concern here, though, is with the religious or theological elements of the poem; and while Johnson is suitably attentive to these, his judgments are uncharacteristically hesitant and even contradictory.

Some of the specifically moral concerns of Johnson's time are difficult for a reader today to entertain. He cites a critic who denounced Milton "for the impiety which sometimes breaks from Satan's mouth," a criticism which makes me wonder what that critic expected to emerge from the mouth of the declared enemy of God, but which Johnson seems to have thought reasonable enough. "For there are thoughts . . . which no observation of character can justify, because no good man would willingly permit them to pass, however transiently, through his own mind." Johnson acquits Milton of the charge while agreeing that the concern is legitimate. "To make Satan speak as a rebel, without any such expressions as might taint the reader's imagination, was indeed one of the great difficulties in Milton's undertaking, and I cannot but think that he has extricated himself with great happiness. There is in Satan's speeches little that can give pain to a pious ear." This seems to me a strange conclusion, in that it seems evident to me that any speech of Satan *should* "give pain to a pious ear"; otherwise such speeches would scarcely be Satanic. But Johnson seems to believe that "no observation of character can justify" portraying Satan as he really is, because exposure to the Adversary's real thoughts would tend to "taint the reader's imagination," something that Johnson cannot countenance.[15] (It would be interesting to overhear a discussion on this subject

15. Johnson, "Life of Milton," pp. 185–86.

between Johnson and, say, Dostoevsky. Or for that matter Milton himself.) For Dr. Johnson, a rich and full exploration of the Satanic psychology is incompatible with the moral obligations of literature.

For Johnson, this is not the only way Milton, for all his undeniable brilliance, has implicated himself in situations that are simply not susceptible to proper literary treatment. In this respect the treatment of Adam and Eve is even more problematic than that of Satan.

On the one hand, Johnson agrees with Addison "that this poem has, by the nature of its subject, the advantage above all others, that it is universally and perpetually interesting. All mankind will, through all ages, bear the same relation to Adam and to Eve, and must partake of that good and evil which extend to themselves." But, on the other hand, he also says: "The plan of *Paradise Lost* has this inconvenience, that it comprises neither human actions nor human manners. The man and woman who act and suffer are in a state which no other man or woman can ever know. The reader finds no transaction in which he can be engaged, beholds no condition in which he can by any effort of imagination place himself; he has, therefore, little natural curiosity or sympathy."[16]

It is not easy to see how these statements can be reconciled with each other: surely a poem which inspires in us "little natural curiosity or sympathy" can scarcely be "universally and perpetually interesting." But perhaps the vast chasm between our spiritual condition and that of Adam and Eve before the Fall, the very fact that the reader "beholds no condition in

16. Johnson, "Life of Milton," pp. 193–94.

which he can by any effort of imagination place himself," is the
very source of perpetual interest. The condition of Adam and
Eve is not the human condition that we know, but this does
not evaporate our interest; rather, it makes that interest *anthropological*. "A state of innocence we can only conceive, if
indeed in our present misery it be possible to conceive it"; and
whether such a conception is possible Johnson does not say.[17]
He leaves it, in the strongest sense of an old phrase, as an exercise for the reader. But he does seem to think it impossible,
for Milton as much as for us, to conceive of it *consistently*. In
the previous chapter I mentioned the problem inherent in
Adam's response to learning that the promised punishment of
disobedience is death: "What e'er death is, / Some dreadful
thing no doubt." It was surely with just such a moment in mind
that Johnson wrote, "To find sentiments for the state of innocence was very difficult; and something of anticipation perhaps is now and then discovered."[18]

17. Johnson, "Life of Milton," p. 192.
18. Johnson, "Life of Milton," p. 199. I should perhaps add that Johnson sometimes criticizes Milton out of plain misunderstanding. For instance, he writes,
"Another inconvenience of Milton's design is that it requires the description of
what cannot be described, the agency of spirits. He saw that immateriality sup-
plied no images, and that he could not show angels acting but by instruments of
action; he therefore invested them with form and matter. This being necessary
was therefore defensible; and he should have secured the consistency of his system by keeping immateriality out of sight, and enticing his reader to drop it from
his thoughts. But he has unhappily perplexed his poetry with his philosophy"
(p. 196). But Milton did not believe that angels are immaterial. They do not have
precisely the same kind of body that human beings do, in his view, but they are
embodied, and in the poem the nature of their embodiment is a matter of interest
to Adam. See V.404ff.

And perhaps Johnson's discourse is at some points inconsistent because his *experience* of reading Milton's poem was variable. Perhaps when he warmly agreed with Addison's judgment that the poem "is universally and perpetually interesting" he was just beginning a reading; because for all his praise of Milton's greatness, in the end he is simply tired and, well, *bored*:

> The want of human interest is always felt. *Paradise Lost* is one of the books which the reader admires and lays down, and forgets to take up again. None ever wished it longer than it is. Its perusal is a duty rather than a pleasure. We read Milton for instruction, retire harassed and overburdened, and look elsewhere for recreation; we desert our master, and seek for companions.[19]

There is of course a kind of praise in this acknowledgment of Milton as "our master," and a kind of humility in the corresponding acknowledgment that we mere readers can't always rise to his level. Johnson's point here is a striking anticipation of something that Virginia Woolf would say a hundred and fifty years later, a judgment we will explore in due course. (It also serves as one of this book's epigraphs.) But while Virginia Woolf was not a Christian, Dr. Johnson was, and one might expect him to have more sympathy for Milton's project. Yet his faith was of a wholly different order from Milton's. Faith for Dr. Johnson was the satisfaction of religious duties rightly performed, pain at the neglect of such

19. Johnson, "Life of Milton," p. 196.

duties, hope for forgiveness and comfort. He was a man of sorrows and acquainted with grief, and was never inclined to minimize his pain or pretend to stoicism; he hoped for a God who is "our refuge and strength, a very present help in trouble" (Psalms 46:1).

Milton's Christianity, by contrast, was almost too large in conception to be described as faith: it was architectural and cosmological, concerned to trace the vast sweep of salvation history. His own sorrows and griefs were great, but he rarely paused to acknowledge them. He was always after a greater prize—the greatest that any poet could aspire to.

———

One more generational hop, to William Cowper, twenty-two years younger than Dr. Johnson. Cowper was also a fascinating figure: a gifted poet, author of several hymns that are still sung today, writer of antislavery poems that were quoted by Martin Luther King Jr.—and a man who for much of his life believed that he was predestined to be damned, a conviction so crushing that more than once he tried to take his own life. He was rescued from his despair largely through the kind ministrations of his friends—including John Newton, the former slave-trader and author of the hymn "Amazing Grace"—who watched over him closely for a number of years. When sane, Cowper was a man of great charm and wit.

Here what matters is his reverence for Milton, which—despite Dr. Johnson's efforts to take the great blind poet down a peg or two—was characteristic of poets of his generation.

Just how reverently Cowper thought of Milton can be easily discerned from a letter he wrote, on 24 February 1793, to his friend William Hayley. It must be quoted at length:

> I dreamed that being in a house in the city, and with much company, looking towards the end of the room from the upper end of it, I descried a figure which I immediately knew to be Milton's. He was very gravely, but very neatly attired in the fashion of his day, and had a countenance which filled me with those feelings that an affectionate child has for a beloved father. . . . My first thought was wonder, where he could have been concealed so many years; my second, a transport of joy to find him still alive; my third, another transport to find myself in his company; and my fourth, a resolution to accost him. I did so, and he received me with a complacence, in which I saw equal sweetness and dignity. I spoke of his *Paradise Lost*, as every man must, who is worthy to speak of it at all, and told him a long story of the manner in which it affected me, when I first discovered it, being at that time a schoolboy. He answered me by a smile, and a gentle inclination of his head. He then grasped my hand affectionately, and with a smile that charmed me, said, 'Well, you for your part will do well also'; at last recollecting his great age (for I understood him to be two hundred years old) I feared that I might fatigue him by much talking, I took my leave, and he took his, with an air of the most perfect good-breeding.[20]

20. William Cowper, *The Letters and Prose Writings: IV: Letters 1792–1799* (Oxford: Oxford University Press, 1979), p. 297.

Cowper was a deeply serious Christian; it is unsurprising that *Paradise Lost* would affect him in this way, and only somewhat surprising that he would have such a dream. (A dream precisely like this one could scarcely be commonplace for anyone.) But Christianity was then losing its formerly central place in British cultural life. Would a later generation—a generation often self-consciously hostile to the Church of England, to orthodox Christianity, often enough to theism itself—have any place for the author of a theologically impassioned poem that takes as historical the biblical account of the Fall of Man?

# 4

# The Devil's Party

AT THE turn of the nineteenth century, the poet who had appeared so charmingly to William Cowper fell from Heaven to earth, to a cottage at Felpham on the Sussex coast: "Then first I saw him in the zenith as a falling star / Descending perpendicular, swift as the swallow or swift."[1] William Blake—poet himself, engraver, visionary—had summoned Milton. He had business to do with his great predecessor.

Blake knows what Milton has been suffering—yes, suffering, in Heaven: "Unhappy though in heaven, he obeyed, he murmured not, he was silent." He had "walked about in Eternity / One hundred years, pondering the intricate mazes of Providence."[2] This is a curious echo of something Milton had written, not about the inhabitants of Heaven but those of

---

1. William Blake, *Milton: A Poem* (Princeton: Princeton University Press, 1998), Plate 15, ll. 46–47. I cite by plate and line number so those using other editions can readily find the quotations, but I have worked from this beautiful edition with fine reproductions of Blake's original illuminations.

2. Blake, *Milton,* Plate 2, ll. 15–17.

FIGURE 4. Frontispiece to William Blake's poem *Milton* (1810).

Hell: as they await the return of "their great Commander" from his mission to earth, they must pass the time.

> Others apart sat on a hill retired,
> In thoughts more elevate, and reasoned high
> Of Providence, Foreknowledge, Will, and Fate—
> Fixed fate, free will, foreknowledge absolute—
> And found no end, in wandering mazes lost.
> Of good and evil much they argued then,
> Of happiness and final misery,
> Passion and apathy, and glory and shame:
> Vain wisdom all, and false philosophy! (II.557–65)

Can those in Heaven lose themselves in "wandering mazes" as those in Hell inevitably do? Only if Satan is right when he says, as he does in one of his first speeches in the poem, "The mind is its own place, and in itself / Can make a Heav'n of Hell, a Hell of Heav'n." And if Heaven has become a Hell for a spirit, how might that spirit be redeemed?

The frontispiece of Blake's *Milton* contains the following words: across the top and right, written partly sideways, *MILTON: A Poem in Two Books*; at the left, also written sideways, *The Author & Printer W. Blake*; and finally across the bottom of the image, *To Justify the Ways of God to Men*. But the title of the poem is undergoing a strange distortion: the *MIL* is being divided from the *TON* by the pressure of a hand, Milton's own hand—Milton portrayed as a heroically muscled nude, facing away from us, looking slightly to his right with a sober expression as his extended right hand forces apart the two syllables of his name and presses into a chaotic background, a whirling pillar of light and darkness.

Is this the moment when he exits his troubled Heaven and begins his fall to earth—a falling that initiates this poem just as the fall of Satan and his followers through chaos initiates *Paradise Lost*? It seems so.

And when his descent takes him to Felpham, he enters the left foot of William Blake—the left foot at the tarsus, Blake emphasizes, the point at which the foot joins the ankle. This seems odd, to say the least; but as Leo Damrosch has pointed out, Blake seems to have thought of the feet as the place where we are joined to the earth, a kind of image of our embodiment, our earthiness.[3] (In a famous lyric from *Milton* Blake writes, "And did those feet in ancient time / Walk upon England's mountains green?"[4]) Moreover, "tarsus" reminds us of Saul of Tarsus, who on the Damascus road saw "a light from heaven" so powerful that it flung him to the ground (Acts 9:3), and Blake shows us an image of himself as Milton's spirit enters his foot: his whole body arcs backwards with the force of the poet's sudden starry arrival. This encounter promises to be transformative for each of these men, both poets, both visionaries, both Londoners.

This poem, like much of Blake's work, is legendarily obscure and difficult, and has as much to say about Blake as about Milton. But we will focus here on the Purgatorial correction the older poet experiences as he dwells within the younger one. It is at least twofold: it is theological and moral, directed at Milton's perverted theology and his cruelty to the women in his

3. Leo Damrosch, *Eternity's Sunrise: The Imaginative World of William Blake* (New Haven: Yale University Press, 2015), p. 211.

4. Blake, *Milton*, Plate 1.

life. Only if these spiritual malformations are corrected, these diseases healed, may Heaven become Heaven for Milton. The remainder of this chapter will unfold this double critique—as it arises in Blake and as it is pursued by others.

———

"Milton was of the Devil's party without knowing it"—one of Blake's most famous statements, and the most famous claim ever made about Milton.[5] Though the sentence names only Satan, it is really a claim about God—the God of *Paradise Lost* and the God of traditional Christian theology. Blake believed that the figure most Christians worship as God is no true God at all, but rather a cosmic tyrant, and a projection of their own worldly desires.

In the last months of his life, Blake read a pamphlet by one Dr. Robert Thornton called *The Lord's Prayer, Newly Translated* (1827), which contains said translation and some commentary. Blake found Thornton's "Tory" interpretation of the prayer contemptible, and decided to make his own translation, one meant to reveal what Thorton really meant and who or what he really worshipped:

> Our Father Augustus Caesar who art in these thy Substantial Astronomical Telescopic Heavens, Holiness to thy Name or Title & reverence to thy Shadow. Thy Kingship come upon Earth first & thence in Heaven. Give us day by

5. From *The Marriage of Heaven and Hell*, in *The Complete Poetry and Prose of William Blake*, rev. ed. (New York: Anchor Books, 1988), p. 35.

day our Real Taxed Substantial Money bought Bread & deliver from the Holy Ghost (so we call Nature) whatever
cannot be Taxed, for all is debts & Taxes between Caesar &
us & one another. Lead us not to read the Bible but let our
Bible be Virgil & Shakspeare & deliver us from Poverty in
Jesus that Evil one. For thine is the Kingship (or Allegoric
Godship) & the Power or War & the Glory or Law Ages
after Ages in thy Descendents, for God is only an Allegory
of Kings & nothing Else. Amen.[6]

For Blake, Dr. Thornton's theology is no real theology at all,
but merely a prop for the existing social order, an elaborate
justification for the Hanoverian monarchy, "for God is only an
Allegory of Kings & nothing Else." One might think that this
particular error is one that Milton, revolutionary and defender
of regicide, would be innocent of, but for Blake there are
strong correspondences between Thornton's God and Milton's. Milton may have wanted us to believe that the God of
*Paradise Lost* is the rightful King of all Creation, but, Blake
thought, Milton did not realize that he had based his God on
human kingship—had created God in the image of the very
kings whose authority over us he denied and denounced.

It was the earthly Milton—the one who departed this
world in 1674—who made such an idol. The beginning of *Milton* suggests that in the subsequent one hundred years, largely
spent "pondering the intricate mazes of Providence," he began
to be transformed into something else—something that
needed to unite, for a time, with William Blake, as Blake

6. *The Complete Poetry and Prose of William Blake*, p. 669.

needed to unite with him. That Milton required such transformation should not be surprising; Blake believed that Jesus did also. Henry Crabb Robinson—who got to know Blake in the last two years of the poet's life and minutely recorded their conversations—wrote that Blake "had been speaking of the errors of Jesus Christ—He was wrong in suffering Himself to be crucified. He should not have attacked the Government. He had no business with such matters. On my inquiring how he reconciled this with the sanctity and divine qualities of Jesus, he said He was not then become the Father."[7]

In Blake's view, all of us—including Jesus of Nazareth—have the greatest difficulty detaching our notions of God from the understandings we acquire as residents of this material world. We get entangled in the concerns of that world and allow them to shape our theology. Just as Jesus lost his way by concerning himself with matters of governance, so too did Dante; indeed, Dante's passionate involvement in Florentine politics marked him as an "atheist." Robinson is puzzled by Blake's use of the term *atheist*; when Milton says that John Locke was an atheist, Robinson points out that Locke both wrote to commend piety and lived a virtuous life, but to Blake this did not seem relevant information. Blake never made his views clearly explicit to Robinson, but he seems to have meant something like this: One whose understanding of God is shaped by the concerns of the material world is an idolater, a worshipper of a false god, a nonexistent God—and therefore,

---

7. Robinson's memoirs of Blake have been reprinted often, but I am citing them as they appear in a kind of appendix to Arthur Symons, *William Blake* (London: Archibald Constable and Company Ltd., 1907), p. 255.

no matter what one's formal profession of faith might be, an atheist. Dante is one, and Locke; Wordsworth too, though a fine poet. (Dante "was the slave of the world and time. But Dante and Wordsworth, in spite of their Atheism, were inspired by the Holy Ghost."[8]) So it should be unsurprising that Blake repeatedly says that Milton was an atheist.

But in the afterlife Milton has learned a few things. Blake often spoke to Robinson about his "visions": "And when he said *my visions* it was in the ordinary unemphatic tone in which we speak of trivial matters that every one understands and cares nothing about."[9] Often, he said, Milton appeared to him: "I saw Milton in imagination, and he told me to beware of being misled by his *Paradise Lost*."[10] Robinson: "Now, according to Blake, Atheism consists in worshipping the natural world, which same natural world, properly speaking, is nothing real, but a mere illusion produced by Satan. Milton was for a great part of his life an Atheist, and therefore has fatal errors in his *Paradise Lost*, which he has often begged Blake to confute."[11] The poem *Milton* is that begged-for confutation.

And it takes the form of a kind of confession. Early in the poem Milton speaks—and here I will quote at some length to give a flavor of Blake's apocalyptic-prophetic voice:

> And Milton said: I go to Eternal Death! The Nations still
> Follow after the detestable Gods of Priam: in pomp
> Of warlike selfhood contradicting and blaspheming.

8. Robinson, in Symons, *William Blake*, pp. 262–63, 274.
9. Robinson, in Symons, *William Blake*, p. 287.
10. Robinson, in Symons, *William Blake*, p. 263.
11. Robinson, in Symons, *William Blake*, p. 274.

When will the Resurrection come to deliver the
    sleeping body From corruptibility; O when, Lord
    Jesus, wilt thou come?
Tarry no longer, for my soul lies at the gates of death.
I will arise and look forth for the morning of the grave:
I will go down to the sepulcher to see if morning breaks:
I will go down to self annihilation and eternal death:
Lest the Last Judgment come & find me unannihilate
And I be seiz'd & giv'n into the hands of my own
    Selfhood.
The Lamb of God is seen thro' mists & shadows,
    hov'ring
Over the sepulchers in clouds of Jehovah & winds of
    Elohim,
A disk of blood distant; & heav'ns & earths roll dark
    between.
What do I here before the Judgment? without my
    Emanation?
With the daughters of memory & not with the
    daughters of inspiration?
I in my Selfhood am that Satan. I am that Evil One![12]

This is Blake's response to the claim that "The mind is its own place." Milton himself had known it to be wrong—that's why he later has Satan say, "Which way I fly is hell; myself am hell" (IV.73)—but because he did not grasp that "Selfhood" is intrinsically Satanic, he suffers the same fate as his story's great antagonist. The difference between the two of

---

12. Blake, *Milton*, Plate 14, ll. 14–30.

them is simply this: Milton still retains the opportunity to learn, and to repent.

For many writers of the Romantic era, Milton is the great predecessor with whom they must reckon, the best example imaginable of Harold Bloom's "anxiety of influence."[13] But, unlike Blake, they are not necessarily reckoning with the poet's theology; some of them are quite beyond that. Charles Lamb, in his lovely essay "Detached Thoughts on Books and Reading" (1822), writes: "Milton almost requires a solemn service of music to be played before you enter upon him. But he brings his music, to which, who listens, had need bring docile thoughts, and purged ears."[14] Music, not theology.

When Keats writes of Milton, as he often does in letters, his terms are strictly literary: "The *Paradise Lost* though so fine in itself is a corruption of our Language—It should be kept as it is unique—a curiosity—a beautiful and grand Curiosity. . . . I have but lately stood on my guard against Milton. Life to him would be death to me."[15] This is purely a matter of being tempted by the grandness of Milton's music; a poet of that era could scarcely have been more thoroughly post-Christian than Keats was.

For Wordsworth the mastery of Milton was something more to be embraced than avoided: Leigh Hunt reports that

13. Harold Bloom, *The Anxiety of Influence: A Theory of Poetry*, 2nd ed. (New York: Oxford University Press, 1997).

14. Charles Lamb, *Selected Prose*, ed. Adam Phillips (London: Penguin, 1985), pp. 151–52.

15. John Keats, *Selected Letters of John Keats, Revised Edition*, ed. Grant F. Scott (Cambridge: Harvard University Press, 2002), p. 379. From one of his journal-letters he wrote for his brother George and George's wife, Georgiana, in America (21 September 1819).

when someone praised the description of honeybees in Shakespeare's *Henry V*—"The singing masons building roofs of gold"—Wordsworth, who didn't like having *-ing* twice in one line, merely said that Milton wouldn't have written it, as though that settled the matter. (The young Keats, ever independent, disagreed: he thought the sound shrewdly mimicked the buzzing of the bees.)[16]

That Wordsworth revered Milton is easily seen in the consistently Miltonic style of his own great long poem, *The Prelude*, which he worked on for much of his adult life. It's a poem with a kind of implicit thesis: That there can an epic of the interior life, a story of personal growth and transformation that—if indeed we all are loved by and belong to (some kind of) God—deserves its own extended poetic treatment, and in a high style. But however magnificent *The Prelude* can be, it is an evasion of the greatest challenges Milton places before us—a changing of the subject rather than a strong reckoning. Its passionately committed interiority neglects the external world—especially the *human* world, which is not as amenable to our fancies as the beauty of Nature.[17]

---

16. Leigh Hunt, *Selected Writings*, ed. David Jesson-Dibley (Milton Park: Taylor & Francis, 2003), p. 108.

17. That said, Wordsworth does tell us in *The Prelude* that the only time in his life he ever got drunk was in Milton's old room in Christ's College, Cambridge:

> Among the band of my compeers was one
> Whom chance had stationed in the very room
> Honoured by Milton's name. O temperate Bard!
> Be it confest that, for the first time, seated
> Within thy innocent lodge and oratory,
> One of a festive circle, I poured out

Blake, though, gives us that strong reckoning, and he did so because he understood the complexly intertwining framework of *Paradise Lost*, its manifold implications, whether pleasant or unpleasant, for the whole of human life. The twentieth-century literary critic Northrop Frye—about whom more in a later chapter—understood the kind of unity for which Blake was always striving, and understood as well the enemies of that unity: "Blake is . . . trying to do for Milton what the prophets and Jesus did for Moses, isolate what is poetic and imaginative, and annihilate what is legal and historical. This is also what he is to do for himself, and there will always be a curse on any critic who tries to see the Christianity and radicalism of Blake as a dichotomy instead of a unity."[18]

Blake grasped the massive implications of Milton's epic architecture in *Paradise Lost*; and so too did four members of the most extraordinary English family of that era: the Godwins and the Shelleys.

———

One cannot understand the fascination of *Paradise Lost* for that strange and marvelous family, or their importance for the

———

Libations, to thy memory drank, till pride
And gratitude grew dizzy in a brain
Never excited by the fumes of wine
Before that hour, or since. (Book III, ll. 296–305)

18. Northrop Frye, *Fearful Symmetry: A Study of William Blake* (Princeton: Princeton University Press, 1947), p. 346.

story I am telling, without appreciating certain key truths about the relationship between religion and politics in their era, and in eras preceding theirs.

Throughout the history of Christian Europe, conflicts between religion and politics repeatedly arise—but even to put the point that way is to mislead. Our terminology cannot be retrojected into the past without confusion arising. Indeed, it is difficult to find a language that is both faithful to the realities and comprehensible to us today. Imagine, then, a single coherent political entity—let us call it Christendom. Let us also say, not wholly arbitrarily, that it begins in Rome on Christmas Day *Anno Domini* 800, when Pope Leo III crowns Charlemagne emperor—something that could happen only because Charlemagne had protected Leo from his enemies and received from the pope a great oath of innocence, a declaration that the many charges those enemies made against him were false. At Rome, hearing testimony in council, Charlemagne declared Leo innocent and banished his enemies. And in return he was named by Leo the successor of the Roman emperors of old.

It would be a gross error to think that Leo represents "religion" and Charlemagne "politics." Charlemagne's declaration in favor of Leo is both religious and political; Leo's crowning of Charlemagne is also—or, it would be better to say, for our modern terms are inadequate, the two men are simply the twin guardians of Christendom, one bearing crown and sword, the other bearing miter and crozier. That Christendom is one interwoven thing—as it would still be centuries later when Charlemagne's successor, Henry IV, walked to Canossa through the snow to prostrate himself before Pope Gregory VII. This is not a conflict between religion and politics in which religion wins; it is a struggle for the proper balance of powers and obligations *within* Christendom.

When, half a millennium later, the Reformation comes, it effectively destroys the idea of Christendom as a single entity, and effectively creates the categories of religion and politics. It could be said that those categories are required as a response to wars between Catholics and Protestants: the Peace of Augsburg in 1555 enshrines the principle of *Cuius regio, eius religio*— "Who rules, his religion." The religion of any given polity is the religion of its prince. And so where one principle, Christendom, had dictated terms, now we have two: *regio* and *religio*. But note that this is by no means the separation of church and state: church and state are one *in any given polity*; the logic of Christendom is thus replicated on a smaller scale. But over the long run this fractal breakage introduced a spirit of division and distinction that could not be controlled: For if Christendom itself can be divided, why not the *idea* of Christendom? Once you have both *regio* and *religio*, why not envision their taking separate and independent paths?

Such separation was resisted in Britain—as can best be seen in the comparatively gentle showing-the-door to King James II in 1688, when his Catholicism threatened to disrupt the delicate balance between the Church of England and the government of king and Parliament. And when the French Revolution broke out in 1789, leading ultimately to a fierce antireligious crusade and the transformation of churches into civic temples—see especially the remaking of the Church of Sainte-Geneviève in Paris into the Panthéon, where the ashes of Voltaire were installed with ceremonial veneration, followed by the bodies of

Rousseau and Marat, among others—British defenders of the *Cuius regio, eius religio* felt quite thoroughly vindicated.

But not all agreed. A number of English radicals saw quite clearly the ways that *religio* supports *regio* even in injustice; becomes, then, a force for repression and the subjugation of the poor and voiceless. And for the Godwins and the Shelleys, the contemplation of these tensions led them with remarkable frequency to the contemplation of *Paradise Lost*.

One of those British figures who felt vindicated by the accelerating violence of the French Revolution was Edmund Burke, the great Anglo-Irish philosopher and statesman whose *Reflections on the Revolution in France* (1790) became the virtual founding document of modern conservatism. It elicited many replies, the first of which—appearing within a month (!)—was *A Vindication of the Rights of Men* by Mary Wollstonecraft, a thirty-one-year-old teacher and governess who was then writing and editing for a London journal called the *Analytical Review*. But Wollstonecraft, whose first book had been *Thoughts on the Education of Daughters* (1787), came quickly to realize that many of the issues she had raised in response to Burke had a particular applicability to the political condition of women. And so she wrote *Vindication of the Rights of Woman* (1792)—in which she was led to thoughts about *Paradise Lost*.

Earlier in this chapter I said that Blake's *Milton* demands of the poet a double reckoning: one with his perverted theology, and the second with his cruelty to women. Scholars have debated and will continue to debate what Milton thought about women and how he treated the women in his life, but Blake had read about how Milton's first wife, Mary Powell, left him

soon after their marriage, thereby prompting his extended demands for the right to divorce; and had read also that he neglected his daughters' education and made sufficiently harsh
demands on them that they rebelled against him; and surely
had wondered how those experiences affected his portrayal of
Eve. Everyone who read English literature at all had read about
Milton and the women in his life—and that includes Mary
Wollstonecraft.

"Women are told from their infancy," she writes, "and taught
by the example of their mothers, that a little knowledge of
human weakness, justly termed cunning, softness of temper,
*outward* obedience, and a scrupulous attention to a puerile
kind of propriety, will obtain for them the protection of man;
and should they be beautiful, every thing else is needless, for,
at least, twenty years of their lives." And she immediate goes
on to note that "Thus Milton describes our first frail mother."[19]
The passage she has in mind we have already seen:

> Two of far nobler shape, erect and tall,
> God-like erect, with native honour clad
> In naked majesty, seemed lords of all,
> And worthy seemed; for in their looks divine
> The image of their glorious Maker shone,
> Truth, wisdom, sanctitude severe and pure—
> Severe, but in true filial freedom placed,
> Whence true authority in men: though both
> Not equal, as their sex not equal seemed;

19. Mary Wollstonecraft, *A Vindication of the Rights of Woman and A Vindication
of the Rights of Men* (Oxford: Oxford University Press, 1993), p. 84.

For contemplation he and valour formed,
For softness she and sweet attractive grace;
He for God only, she for God in him. (IV.288–99)

Milton is the chief major writer she thinks of as teaching this doctrine of feminine docility—"though when he tells us that women are formed for softness and sweet attractive grace, I cannot comprehend his meaning, unless, in the true Mahometan strain, he meant to deprive us of souls, and insinuate that we were beings only designed by sweet attractive grace, and docile blind obedience, to gratify the senses of man when he can no longer soar on the wing of contemplation."[20] And indeed, as we have seen, Milton does explicitly say that Adam was formed "for God only," Eve "for God in him"—Wollstonecraft is not reading him uncharitably.

She passes on from this comment, but Milton keeps coming back to her mind, like the personification of a toothache. (As Sandra Gilbert and Susan Gubar have noted, "*A Vindication of the Rights of Woman* often reads like an outraged commentary on *Paradise Lost*."[21]) Later in the same chapter, as she writes about the distinctive variety of mutual affection between husband and wife that she often hears praised, she pauses to comment: "yet, has not the sight of this moderate felicity excited more tenderness than respect? An emotion similar to what we feel when children are playing, or animals sporting." That final word is accompanied by a footnote which returns us to *Para-*

20. Wollstonecraft, *Vindication*, p. 84.
21. Sandra Gilbert and Susan Gubar, *The Madwoman in the Attic: The Woman Writer and the Nineteenth-Century Literary Imagination* (New Haven: Yale University Press, 1979), p. 205.

*dise Lost*: "Similar feelings has Milton's pleasing picture of paradisiacal happiness ever raised in my mind; yet, instead of envying the lovely pair, I have, with conscious dignity, or Satanic pride, turned to hell for sublimer objects."[22] *Call me Satanic if you will*, she says, *I prefer nobler forms of love than Milton offers in his scenes of Edenic domestic tranquility.*

And indeed, she continues in a more convoluted passage, this response is consistent with her general aesthetic preferences: "when viewing some noble monument of human art, I have traced the emanation of the Deity in the order I admired"—that is, she has asked herself what, specifically, in the form and character of a work she finds divine, sublime—"till, descending from that giddy height, I have caught myself contemplating the grandest of all human sights;—for fancy quickly placed, in some solitary recess, an outcast of fortune, rising superior to passion and discontent."[23] Nothing more powerfully moves her, nothing is more grand and high, than such an "outcast of fortune" who nevertheless transcends any feeling of mere "discontent," who is never captive to mere "passion." Might not Milton's Satan—an outcast indeed, and one who rejoices in the possession of "A mind not to be changed by place or time" (I.253)—fairly meet this description?

Just over a year after the publication of Wollstonecraft's book, another writer, William Godwin, also moved by the complex spectacle of the revolution in France, published *An Enquiry Concerning Political Justice*, a book of political philosophy in which he too meditates on *Paradise Lost*, and especially

22. Wollstonecraft, *Vindication*, p. 426.
23. Wollstonecraft, *Vindication*, p. 84.

on Satan. At one point in his exposition he asks a question: "Can great intellectual energy exist without a strong sense of justice?" And his answer begins with a curious swerve into the Miltonic landscape:

> It has no doubt resulted from a train of speculation similar to this, that poetical readers have commonly remarked Milton's devil to be a being of considerable virtue. It must be admitted that his energies centered too much in personal regards. But why did he rebel against his maker? It was, as he himself informs us, because he saw no sufficient reason for that extreme inequality of rank and power which the creator assumed. It was because prescription and precedent form no adequate ground for implicit faith. After his fall, why did he still cherish the spirit of opposition? From a persuasion that he was hardly and injuriously treated. He was not discouraged by the apparent inequality of the contest: because a sense of reason and justice was stronger in his mind, than a sense of brute force: because he had much of the feelings of an Epictetus or a Cato, and little of those of a slave. He bore his torments with fortitude, because he disdained to be subdued by despotic power. He sought revenge, because he could not think with tameness of the unexpostulating authority that assumed to dispose of him. How beneficial and illustrious might the temper from which these qualities flowed have proved with a small diversity of situation![24]

This is interestingly ambivalent, and on some matters reticent. Godwin has to admit that Satan's "energies centered too much

---

24. William Godwin, *An Enquiry Concerning Political Justice* (Oxford: Oxford University Press, 2013), p. 143.

in personal regards," but this concession made, he waxes lyrical about the character's many virtues: driven by "a sense of reason and justice," he was undaunted by an opponent more powerful than he; he would be like Cato, who famously took his own life rather than submit to tyranny. Well—*Satan* thinks God's authority over him tyrannous ("he saw no sufficient reason for that extreme inequality of rank and power which the creator assumed"), but this is a point Godwin neither endorses nor rejects. Godwin seems to think of Milton's Satan as someone caught in an unfortunate situation not of his own making: had his position been even slightly less exposed to temptation, "How beneficial and illustrious might the temper from which these qualities flowed have proved." Indeed, Godwin follows Dryden in naming Satan as the hero of *Paradise Lost*, and not merely in the sense of being the chief character: immediately after the passage I have just quoted, he notes that

> A man of quick resentment, of strong feelings, and who pertinaciously resists every thing that he regards as an unjust assumption, may be considered as having in him the seeds of eminence. Nor is it easily to be conceived that such a man should not proceed from a sense of justice to some degree of benevolence; as Milton's hero felt real compassion and sympathy for his partners in misfortune.[25]

I see no evidence of Satan's compassion for his fellow rebels, but Godwin did, and adds it to his extensive list of the virtues of "Milton's hero." Like Wollstonecraft, he does not openly *reject* the Christian understanding of the Bible's first story; but

25. Godwin, *Enquiry*, p. 144.

both of them strongly suggest that it is a story about which divergent views may legitimately be held.

In January of 1796—three years after the publication of *An Enquiry Concerning Political Justice*, and four after the appearance of *Vindication of the Rights of Woman*—Wollstonecraft and Godwin met at a friend's house in London. By August they were lovers; the following February they married; in August of that year Wollstonecraft gave birth to their daughter, Mary. Ten days later she was dead.

———

Godwin grieved; but eventually he recovered himself sufficiently to resume his career as a writer of drama, fiction, and polemic. In 1805 he remarried, and he and his second wife, Mary Jane Clairmont, ran a bookshop for children, of all things, in the Strand; but he was constantly in financial straits for the rest of his life. In 1812 he received a letter from a young poet who adored the *Enquiry Concerning Political Justice* and proclaimed himself Godwin's faithful disciple. ("The name of Godwin has been used to excite in me feelings of reverence and admiration, I have been accustomed to consider him a luminary too dazzling for the darkness which surrounds him, and from the earliest period of my knowledge of his principles. I have ardently desired to share on the footing of intimacy that intellect which I have been delighted to contemplate in its emanations."[26]) Percy Shelley

———

26. William St. Clair, *The Godwins and the Shelleys: The Biography of a Family* (London: Faber, 1989), pp. 313–14. St. Clair is my chief guide to the lives of this remarkable family.

apparently had believed Godwin to be dead until informed otherwise by Robert Southey. Shelley was nineteen years old, married a year earlier to Harriet Westbrook, and the author of, among other things, a pamphlet called *The Necessity of Atheism* that, with his friend Thomas Jefferson Hogg, he had written as a student at Oxford. This might have been forgivable, or even unnoticed, except that Shelley mailed copies of the pamphlet to every bishop in the Church of England and the heads of all the Oxford colleges. Expulsion of Shelley and Hogg quickly followed, which was probably what Shelley wanted.

The dedication of his powers to the radical politics of Godwin was a decisive step into political maturity; presumably he did not know that it would lead to an affair with Godwin's sixteen-year-old daughter, Mary. On 26 June 1814, they confessed their love for each other while visiting Mary Wollstonecraft's grave in St. Pancras Churchyard, and soon thereafter ran away to Switzerland. In late 1616 Harriet Shelley, pregnant by a lover she believed had abandoned her, drowned herself in the Serpentine in Hyde Park. She was twenty-one. Shelley disclaimed any responsibility for Harriet's death and blamed her family. He and Mary Godwin immediately married. And in Switzerland, two years later, the couple's serious contemplation of Milton began—one more extensive and more imaginative than that of their elders.

If you could conjure Blake's instinctive repulsion from Milton's theology while banishing Blake's esoteric metaphysics, you might get someone like Percy Shelley. He thought constantly about *Paradise Lost*, and most especially about Milton's Satan. It appears that Shelley may have contemplated a poem featuring

Satan: in his preface to his verse drama *Prometheus Unbound* (1820) he compares his chosen hero, Prometheus, with Satan:

> The only imaginary being, resembling in any degree Prometheus, is Satan; and Prometheus is, in my judgment, a more poetical character than Satan, because, in addition to courage, and majesty, and firm and patient opposition to omnipotent force, he is susceptible of being described as exempt from the taints of ambition, envy, revenge, and a desire for personal aggrandizement, which, in the hero of *Paradise Lost*, interfere with the interest.

Like his father-in-law and mentor, then, he acknowledges that Satan—the evident "hero" of Milton's poem—is a flawed character. The conclusions he draws from this imperfection are fascinating: "The character of Satan engenders in the mind a pernicious casuistry which leads us to weigh his faults with his wrongs, and to excuse the former because the latter exceed all measure." Shelley thus attributes "casuistry" not to Satan but rather to the readers of *Paradise Lost*: we tend to excuse Satan's faults because we see how terribly he has been wronged. Note that Shelley expects his readers to have the same disdain for Christianity that he does and therefore the same sympathy for Satan—the same *excessive* sympathy: because Milton has made him too attractive, we readers are too forgiving of Satan. Shelley then, as though suddenly recalling that Christians still walked the earth, adds that "In the minds of those who consider that magnificent fiction *Paradise Lost* with a religious feeling the portrayal of Satan engenders something worse." The "something worse" is presumably a complete rejection of Satan. Such a tangle of mixed feelings, admiration mixed with a felt need to condemn, can be avoided by selecting another heroic rebel as one's protagonist: "Prometheus is, as it were, the type of the highest perfection of moral and intellectual nature impelled by the purest and the truest motives to the best and noblest ends."[27] Q.E.D.

But Shelley wasn't finished with Milton or his Satan. Soon after publishing *Prometheus Unbound* Shelley returned to the topic in an essay called "On the Devil, and Devils": "Milton so far violated all that part of the popular creed which is susceptible of being preached and defended in argument, as to allege no superiority in moral virtue to his God over his Devil." This juxtaposition of two complex and heroic characters, Satan and God, the first more admirable than the second, testifies to Milton's greatness: "The writer who would have attributed majesty and beauty to the character of victorious and vindictive omnipotence, must have been contented with the character of a good Christian; he never could have been a great epic poet." But that particular form of literary excellence also makes Shelley question—in a manner not altogether unlike Samuel Johnson when he deprecated Milton's failure to pray—Milton's actual religious commitments:

It is difficult to determine, in a country where the most enormous sanctions of opinion and law are attached to a direct avowal of certain speculative notions, whether Milton was

27. Percy Shelley, *Selected Poems and Prose*, ed. Jack Donovan and Cian Duffy (London: Penguin, 2016), pp. 184–85.

a Christian or not, at the period of the composition of *Paradise Lost*. . . . Thus much is certain, that Milton gives the Devil all imaginable advantage; and the arguments with which he exposes the injustice and impotent weakness of his adversary, are such as, had they been printed, distinct from the shelter of any dramatic order, would have been answered by the most conclusive of syllogisms—persecution.

Surely Shelley is here thinking of his own expulsion from Oxford when he had been so bold as to challenge theism directly, without "the shelter of any dramatic order." He seems almost to imagine Milton as what he himself would have been had he been born two hundred years earlier. "The Devil owes everything to Milton. Dante and Tasso present us with a very gross idea of him. Milton divested him of a sting, hoof, and horns, and clothed him with the sublime grandeur of a graceful but tremendous spirit."[28]

And a year later, in one of his last major works—he would drown in the Ligurian Sea in July 1822—Shelley returned yet again to the theme. In his powerful "Defense of Poetry" (1821) he writes, "Nothing can exceed the energy and magnificence of the character of Satan as expressed in *Paradise Lost*. It is a mistake to suppose that he could ever have been intended for the popular personification of evil." This is very cleverly done, as much as to say: *Of the Devil's party without knowing it? Why, he knew perfectly well what he was doing*:

> Milton's Devil as a moral being is as far superior to his God, as one who perseveres in some purpose which he has

28. Shelley, *Selected Poems and Prose*, p. 632.

conceived to be excellent in spite of adversity and torture, is to one who in the cold security of undoubted triumph inflicts the most horrible revenge upon his enemy, not from any mistaken notion of inducing him to repent of a perseverance in enmity, but with the alleged design of exasperating him to deserve new torments. Milton has so far violated the popular creed (if this shall be judged to be a violation) as to have alleged no superiority of moral virtue to his God over his Devil. And this bold neglect of a direct moral purpose is the most decisive proof of the supremacy of Milton's genius.[29]

Shelley likes to give Milton the benefit of the doubt: "the sacred Milton was, let it ever be remembered, a republican and a bold inquirer into morals and religion," and if his consciously held views did not make their way to atheism—atheism in Shelley's sense, not Blake's—he pointed his descendants in the right direction. "We owe to the great writers of the golden age of our literature," chief among them Milton, "that fervid awakening of the public mind which shook to dust the oldest and most oppressive form of the Christian religion." Now it is time for the next step: "The great writers of our own age are, we have reason to suppose, the companions and forerunners of some unimagined change in our social condition or the opinions which cement it."[30] The change may be as yet "unimagined" by most, but we rightly suspect that Shelley has imagined it: what's left of Christianity must be shaken to dust

29. Shelley, *Selected Poems and Prose*, p. 668.
30. Shelley, *Selected Poems and Prose*, p. 186.

as its "oldest and most oppressive form" was shaken by Milton and his contemporaries.

———

Almost all that I have quoted from Percy Shelley was written in England; but earlier I wrote that his and Mary's serious contemplation of Milton began in Switzerland. Why? Because of *Frankenstein*. This is not to say that Percy Shelley did not read Milton before his wife wrote that book; but I think her tale provided the wellspring of his later thoughts—the thoughts I have just explored.

In an introduction to an 1831 reprinting of *Frankenstein*, Mary Wollstonecraft Shelley described the book's genesis: "In the summer of 1816, we visited Switzerland, and became the neighbours of Lord Byron. At first we spent our pleasant hours on [Lake Geneva], or wandering on its shores. . . . But it proved a wet, ungenial summer, and incessant rain often confined us for days to the house."[31] This was the infamous "year without a summer," the world's skies having been darkened by debris ejected in the eruption of Indonesia's Mount Tambora the previous April—the most powerful eruption ever recorded by humans, and the cause of famines around the world, as crops failed to grow in the cold darkness. "Some volumes of ghost stories, translated from the German into French, fell into our hands," and Lord Byron proposed that each person present—Byron himself, his friend John Polidori, and the

———

31. Mary Shelley, *Frankenstein: or, the Modern Prometheus* (London: Penguin, 1992), p. 6.

Shelleys—write their own ghostly tale. This was an opportunity for Mary Shelley to begin the achievement of something she had long contemplated: "It is not singular that, as the daughter of two persons of distinguished literary celebrity, I should very early in life have thought of writing."[32] But up to that point no appropriate subject had occurred to her. Then:

> Many and long were the conversations between Lord Byron and Shelley, to which I was a devout but nearly silent listener. During one of these, various philosophical doctrines were discussed, and among others the nature of the principle of life, and whether there was any probability of its ever being discovered and communicated. . . . Perhaps a corpse would be re-animated; galvanism had given token of such things: perhaps the component parts of a creature might be manufactured, brought together, and endued with vital warmth.

And, lying in bed that night, "I saw the hideous phantasm of a man stretched out, and then, on the working of some powerful engine, show signs of life, and stir with an uneasy, half vital motion."[33] Her tale had begun. It was her husband, she says, who encouraged her to make it a novel, not just a short story; but she wrote it all herself.

The title page of the first edition of the novel (figure 5) features as its epigraph a pair of questions asked in *Paradise Lost*. It is vital to establish the context of these questions Shelley extracts from the poem. At the end of Book IX Adam and Eve have both eaten "the sacred fruit forbidden," and have thus

32. Shelley, *Frankenstein*, p. 5.
33. Shelley, *Frankenstein*, p. 8.

# FRANKENSTEIN;

OR,

## THE MODERN PROMETHEUS.

---◆---

IN THREE VOLUMES,

---◆---

Did I request thee, Maker, from my clay
To mould me man?   Did 1 solicit thee
From darkness to promote me?——
PARADISE LOST.

FIGURE 5. Part of the title page of the first
edition of Mary Shelley's *Frankenstein*.

entered into a giddy spiral of emotion: excitement, "dalliance,"
lust, shame, and, ultimately, "mutual accusation": the final line
of that book is "And of their vain contest appeared no end."
Book X then begins with a series of brief scenes:

1. In Heaven, God the Father reminds the assembled
   angelic council that he told them this would happen,
   and has prescribed the remedy.
2. The Son descends to earth—this is a distinctive version
   of the events described in Genesis 3:8–24—to pronounce judgment on Adam and Eve and exile them
   from Eden.
3. At the gates of Hell, Sin and Death wait, rather bored it
   seems, but their boredom is relieved when Satan

appears to boast of his great achievement, and invite
them to head earthward to take their pleasure: "You
two this way . . . right down to Paradise descend."

4. Continuing on to Hell proper, Satan boasts of his
victory, only to find himself "punished in the shape he
sinned"; and likewise his followers "were all transformed / Alike, to serpents as all accessories / To his
bold riot."

5. Sin and Death rejoice in their new happy hunting
ground. God the Father, watching from Heaven, reminds
his court that they will ultimately be defeated; but for
now they run riot, and with the daughter of Sin, Discord,
bring misery to the whole of this newly-created world.

Which brings us back to Adam, who sits in the midst of the
chaos and misery, "in sorrow abandoned," "in a troubled sea
of passion tossed," and begins an extraordinary soliloquy. This
is not one of the most famous moments in *Paradise Lost*, but
I think it is one of the greatest—a soliloquy that in its elo-
quence, its emotional complexity, and its storms of contradictory thoughts, rivals the best of Shakespeare. Adam oscillates
among shame, guilt, grief, anger, despair, and—this is key for
our purposes here—resentment at God for having put him in
this situation. Not, to be sure, for punishing him for his sin: if
it is God's purpose to "hide me from the face / Of God, whom
to behold was then my height / Of happiness," that would be
clearly right and just: "I deserved it, and would bear / My own
deservings." All that would be "well, if here would end / The
misery"; but it doesn't end there. He looks around him and he
sees an entire world dragged now into discord and pain and

death, and, he thinks "this will not serve: / All that I eat or drink, or shall beget, / Is propagated curse" (X.724–29). And it is this inevitable and ongoing "propagated curse," these endlessly expanding concentric circles of misery, that prompt him to ask the question Mary Shelley quotes:

> Did I request thee, Maker, from my clay
> To mould me man, did I solicit thee
> From darkness to promote me . . . ? (X.743–45)

He then argues with himself on these matters, weaving back and forth from point to counterpoint. Any attempt to describe the soliloquy makes it sound more rationally sequential than it is, but perhaps the most prominent of Adam's thoughts are these:

> Be it so, for I submit; his doom is fair,
> That dust I am, and shall to dust return.
> O welcome hour whenever! Why delays
> His hand to execute what his decree
> Fixed on this day? Why do I overlive,
> Why am I mocked with death, and lengthened out
> To deathless pain? How gladly would I meet
> Mortality my sentence, and be earth
> Insensible! How glad would lay me down
> As in my mother's lap! There I should rest,
> And sleep secure; his dreadful voice no more
> Would thunder in my ears; no fear of worse
> To me, and to my offspring, would torment me
> With cruel expectation. (X.769–82)

Why would he think it worthwhile to live in *this* condition?

In Mary Shelley's novel, the creature, as everyone knows, escapes from his master and flees into the Swiss countryside, where he learns that human beings are terrified of him; so he hides himself in the woods, only occasionally sneaking out to observe these strange folk, folk of one being with his maker. By regularly eavesdropping on a local family of cottagers he acquires the rudiments of a human language, though of course he dares not reveal himself to them.

But then, one day, he enters a great new era of his life: it begins when he "found on the ground a leathern portmanteau containing several articles of dress and some books." What books? "They consisted of *Paradise Lost*, a volume of Plutarch's *Lives*, and the *Sorrows of Werther*." Only the third—the 1774 novel that had made Goethe famous—was recent. "The possession of these treasures gave me extreme delight; I now continually studied and exercised my mind upon these histories, whilst my friends were employed in their ordinary occupations."[34]

All three books fascinate the creature,

> But *Paradise Lost* excited different and far deeper emotions. I read it, as I had read the other volumes which had fallen into my hands, as a true history. It moved every feeling of wonder and awe that the picture of an omnipotent God warring with his creatures was capable of exciting. I often referred the several situations, as their similarity struck me, to my own. Like Adam, I was apparently united by no link

34. Shelley, *Frankenstein*, p. 124.

to any other being in existence; but his state was far different from mine in every other respect. He had come forth from the hands of God a perfect creature, happy and prosperous, guarded by the especial care of his Creator; he was allowed to converse with and acquire knowledge from beings of a superior nature, but I was wretched, helpless, and alone. Many times I considered Satan as the fitter emblem of my condition, for often, like him, when I viewed the bliss of my protectors, the bitter gall of envy rose within me.[35]

There is even a sense in which the creature is a kind of anti-Eve: for Eve, before she meets Adam, grows fascinated with the beauty of her own image in a pond, while the creature's experience is quite the opposite: "I had admired the perfect forms of my cottagers—their grace, beauty, and delicate complexions; but how was I terrified when I viewed myself in a transparent pool! At first I started back, unable to believe that it was indeed I who was reflected in the mirror; and when I became fully convinced that I was in reality the monster that I am, I was filled with the bitterest sensations of despondence and mortification. Alas! I did not yet entirely know the fatal effects of this miserable deformity."[36] Those effects being their dread and horror when they finally see their benefactor, whom they had believed to be a "good spirit."

From this point on in the story *Paradise Lost* becomes a constant shadow of the creature's story, a narrative of a small number of exemplary figures, in any one of which he might

35. Shelley, *Frankenstein*, p. 126.
36. Shelley, *Frankenstein*, p. 110.

discern himself. The only character missing: a Savior, a Redeemer—one willing and able to mend the broken world.

When he realizes that he is more agile and more powerful than Victor Frankenstein, and could easily kill him or anyone he loves, the creature even assumes the power of God—or *a* power, one such power: the power to kill. He does not have the power to make new life. And so, miserable and alone, he turns to his maker for assistance:

> "What I ask of you is reasonable and moderate; I demand a creature of another sex, but as hideous as myself; the gratification is small, but it is all that I can receive, and it shall content me. It is true, we shall be monsters, cut off from all the world; but on that account we shall be more attached to one another. Our lives will not be happy, but they will be harmless and free from the misery I now feel. Oh! My creator, make me happy; let me feel gratitude towards you for one benefit! Let me see that I excite the sympathy of some existing thing; do not deny me my request!"[37]

Note that he first *asks* and then *demands* and then *requests*; he is a humble penitent (like Adam), then a threatening power (like God), then he reverts to deference. Victor Frankenstein—who has assumed the powers of a God without even seeking, much less gaining, the appropriate wisdom—cannot reckon with these oscillations. The creature says, "I swear to you, by the earth which I inhabit, and by you that made me, that with the companion you bestow, I will quit the neighbourhood of man and dwell, as it may chance, in the most savage of places.

37. Shelley, *Frankenstein*, p. 141.

My evil passions will have fled, for I shall meet with sympathy! My life will flow quietly away, and in my dying moments I shall not curse my maker"[38]—but Victor does not know whether to trust him. He *does not know what he has made*. He is more like Adam, appalled and flummoxed by the consequences of his actions, than like an omnipotent deity.

But he does not do his creature's will; and that creature begins a campaign of terror which ends with the killing—almost euthanasia, given the mental and physical decline that Victor Frankenstein has suffered—of his creator. Standing over Frankenstein's body, the creature cries, "In his murder my crimes are consummated; the miserable series of my being is wound to its close! Oh, Frankenstein! Generous and self-devoted being! What does it avail that I now ask thee to pardon me? I, who irretrievably destroyed thee by destroying all thou lovedst. Alas! He is cold, he cannot answer me."[39]

To Robert Walton, whose letters tell this tale and who hears this speech, the miserable one tries to explain himself: "My heart was fashioned to be susceptible of love and sympathy, and when wrenched by misery to vice and hatred, it did not endure the violence of the change without torture such as you cannot even imagine." When he decides that he must kill Elizabeth, Victor's beloved, he says, "I knew that I was preparing for myself a deadly torture, but I was the slave, not the master, of an impulse which I detested yet could not disobey. Yet when she died! Nay, then I was not miserable. I had cast off all feeling, subdued all anguish, to riot in the excess of my

38. Shelley, *Frankenstein*, p. 142.
39. Shelley, *Frankenstein*, p. 211.

THE DEVIL'S PARTY 121

despair. Evil thenceforth became my good."[40] This is of course a near-quotation from *Paradise Lost*: When in Book IV Satan considers the possibility of repentance for his sins, and realizes that repentance requires "submission," he knows that he has no way back:

> So farewell hope; and with hope farewell fear;
> Farewell, remorse: all good to me is lost;
> Evil, be thou my good . . . (IV.108–10)

That it would come to this, or something like this, the creature foresaw early on. Much earlier, when he first sought out Frankenstein and poured out to him the story of his brief life, he had begun with a kind of inadvertent prophecy:

> "I am thy creature, and I will be even mild and docile to my natural lord and king if thou wilt also perform thy part, the which thou owest me. Oh, Frankenstein, be not equitable to every other and trample upon me alone, to whom thy justice, and even thy clemency and affection, is most due. Remember that I am thy creature; I ought to be thy Adam, but I am rather the fallen angel, whom thou drivest from joy for no misdeed. Everywhere I see bliss, from which I alone am irrevocably excluded. I was benevolent and good; misery made me a fiend. Make me happy, and I shall again be virtuous."[41]

Like Milton's Adam, he says: *Without my permission, you made me; you should then make me happy.* And thus the eternal cycle

---

40. Shelley, *Frankenstein*, p. 212.
41. Shelley, *Frankenstein*, pp. 96–97.

of recrimination begins: the creator says, "If you are virtuous, you will be happy"; the creature replies, "If I were happy, I would be virtuous." Both alike seem befuddled by what St. Paul called "the mystery of iniquity" (2 Thessalonians 2:7)—a mystery, it seems to Percy and Mary Shelley, most vividly presented to us in the verse of *Paradise Lost*, and a mystery with no evident resolution. "And of their vain contest appeared no end."

# 5

# Proxy Wars

AS THE nineteenth century progressed, engagements with *Paradise Lost* as a great force to be reckoned with still occurred, but they grew increasingly rare, and they tended to echo the Romantics' interpretations of Milton. For instance, Charlotte Brontë's *Shirley* (1849) features a passionate denunciation of Milton's Eve and argues for replacing her with a kind of nature goddess; the writing is vibrant, but the ideas largely recapitulate Mary Wollstonecraft's contempt for Milton's picture of the first woman.[1] George Meredith's sonnet "Lucifer in

1. Shirley denounces Milton to her friend Caroline: "Milton was great; but was he good? Milton tried to see the first woman; but, Cary, he saw her not. . . . It was his cook that he saw" (Charlotte Brontë, *Shirley* [Harmondsworth: Penguin, 1974], p. 314). Eve, Shirley contends in opposition to the poet, was a female Titan:

> Her robe of blue air spreads to the outskirts of the heath, where yonder flock is grazing; a veil white as an avalanche sweeps from her head to her feet, and arabesques of lightning flame on its borders. Under her breast I see her zone, purple like that horizon; through its blush shines the star of evening. Her steady eyes I cannot picture. They are clear, they are deep as lakes, they are lifted and full of worship, they tremble with the softness of love and the lustre of prayer. Her forehead has the expanse of a cloud, and

FIGURE 6. William Blake, *The Temptation and Fall of Eve*, from his illustrations of *Paradise Lost* (1808).

Starlight" (1883) picks up from sympathetic commentators of the Romantic era an image of a powerful Satan who is nevertheless helpless against "the armies of unalterable law." It is surely Milton's portrayal of the Adversary he has in mind, as in a thoroughly Shelleyan fashion he outlines a condensed symbol of noble but futile resistance to a massively powerful moral order.[2]

But these were very much minority engagements. The more common view of *Paradise Lost* in the Victorian era is illustrated by Mark Twain in his "Address at the Dinner of the Nineteenth Century Club," 1900:

---

is paler than the early moon, risen long before dark gathers. She reclines her bosom on the ridge of Stilbro' Moor; her mighty hands are joined beneath it. So kneeling, face to face she speaks with God. That Eve is Jehovah's daughter, as Adam was His son.

Caroline is not impressed: "She is very vague and visionary. Come, Shirley, we ought to go into church" (p. 316).

2. The poem is truly wonderful, though, and in a distinctly Miltonic register:

On a starred night Prince Lucifer uprose.
Tired of his dark dominion swung the fiend
Above the rolling ball in cloud part screened,
Where sinners hugged their spectre of repose.
Poor prey to his hot fit of pride were those.
And now upon his western wing he leaned,
Now his huge bulk o'er Afric's sands careened,
Now the black planet shadowed Arctic snows.
Soaring through wider zones that pricked his scars
With memory of the old revolt from Awe,
He reached a middle height, and at the stars,
Which are the brain of heaven, he looked, and sank.
Around the ancient track marched, rank on rank,
The army of unalterable law.

Professor Winchester also said something about there being no modern epics like *Paradise Lost*. I guess he's right. He talked as if he was pretty familiar with that piece of literary work, and nobody would suppose that he never had read it. I don't believe any of you have ever read *Paradise Lost*, and you don't want to. That's something that you just want to take on trust. It's a classic, just as Professor Winchester says, and it meets his definition of a classic—something that everybody wants to have read and nobody wants to read.[3]

Generally speaking, the Victorian era proved to be one that domesticated or marginalized *Paradise Lost*. This occurred in two ways. First, many Victorians are less interested in the poetry and more interested in the person of John Milton. Perhaps the most vivid example of this is Thomas Babington Macaulay's long essay—pre-Victorian, to be precise: it appeared in 1825, but anticipates the Miltonic future—in which he celebrates "in all love and reverence, the genius and virtues of John Milton, the poet, the statesman, the philosopher, the glory of English literature, the champion and the martyr of English liberty"—not primarily because Milton was a great poet but rather because he was in a sense the first Whig, the first person to articulate an antimonarchical politics in terms that would be recognizable and appealing to Victorian liberals like Macaulay's readers. "It is by his poetry that Milton is best known"; but it is more important to affirm that of liberal

3. *The Complete Works of Mark Twain*, vol. 24, *Mark Twain's Speeches* (New York: Harper and Brothers, 1923), p. 210.

principles "Milton was the most devoted and eloquent literary champion." And more:

> There are a few characters which have stood the closest scrutiny and the severest tests, which have been tried in the furnace and have proved pure, which have been weighed in the balance and have not been found wanting, which have been declared sterling by the general consent of mankind, and which are visibly stamped with the image and superscription of the Most High. These great men we trust that we know how to prize; and of these was Milton.[4]

For Macaulay, Milton is a great poet; but it scarcely matters that he was: the poetic achievement discreetly recedes in favor of the Great Public Man.

If Macaulay marginalizes *Paradise Lost*, other Victorian public intellectuals domesticate it, by treating it as one among many classics of English literature; they grant it a comforting canonical familiarity. This can most clearly be seen in Matthew Arnold's lecture in February 1888 at the dedication of memorial windows to Milton at St. Margaret's Church, Westminster.[5] Perhaps the best way to understand Arnold's lecture is as a counterweight to Macaulay's, for Arnold insists that

---

4. There are many readily available public-domain editions of Macaulay's *Critical and Historical Essays*, and most of them begin with this portrait of Milton, which Macaulay himself seems to have thought the piece in which he most clearly and forcefully stakes out his core convictions.

5. It proved to be Arnold's last public lecture: he died two months later. Archdeacon Frederic Farrar of Westminster Abbey had deplored the dearth of memorials to Milton in London, and made an appeal for funds that was answered by the American philanthropist George W. Childs. St. Margaret's Church was deemed the

The Milton of religious and political controversy, and perhaps of domestic life also, is not seldom disfigured by want of amenity, by acerbity. The Milton of poetry, on the other hand, is one of those great men "who are modest"—to quote a fine remark of Leopardi . . . —"who are modest, because they continually compare themselves, not with other men, but with that idea of the perfect which they have before their mind." The Milton of poetry is the man, in his own magnificent phrase, of "devout prayer to that Eternal Spirit that can enrich with all utterance and knowledge, and sends out his Seraphim with the hallowed fire of his altar, to touch and purify the lips of whom he pleases."

If for Macaulay Milton's greatness is essentially political and only secondarily poetic, Arnold reverses the polarity. It is the greatness of Milton's verse that truly matters.

So, by the last decades of the nineteenth century, Milton's stature as a great writer was unquestionable and the place of *Paradise Lost* among the classics of English literature could not be doubted; but the poem had ceased to be one that people felt it necessary personally to reckon with, and cer-

---

best location, because Milton had worshipped there when he worked as Secretary for Foreign Tongues, had married Katherine Woodcock there, and had buried her and their infant daughter there. It was thought that, since an American paid for the window, an American poet might be recruited to write a verse for it, and John Greenleaf Whittier obliged:

> The New World honours him whose lofty plea
> For England's freedom made her own more sure,
> Whose song, immortal as its theme, shall be
> Their common freehold while both worlds endure.

tainly there was no need to reckon with it in specifically *religious* terms.

Indeed, it had become so firmly fixed a planet in the canonical firmament that a reader could readily confess, at least to herself, its complete lack of relevance and interest. Thus Virginia Woolf's diary entry from 1918, which deserves to be quoted at some length:

> I am struck by the extreme difference between this poem and any other. It lies, I think, in the sublime aloofness and impersonality of the emotion. I have never read Cowper on the sofa, but I can imagine that the sofa is a degraded substitute for *Paradise Lost*. The substance of Milton is all made of wonderful, beautiful, and masterly descriptions of angels' bodies, battles, flights, dwelling places. He deals in horror and immensity and squalor and sublimity but never in the passions of the human heart. Has any great poem ever let in so little light upon one's own joys and sorrows? I get no help in judging life; I scarcely feel that Milton lived or knew men and women; except for the peevish personalities about marriage and the woman's duties. He was the first of the masculinists, but his disparagement rises from his own ill luck and seems even a spiteful last word in his domestic quarrels.

And yet, having noted how lamentably "masculinist" Milton is—we should recall that by this point his mistreatment of the women in his life had been a standard theme of discourse about Milton for more than a hundred years—Woolf rushes on to confess that this is not the only, perhaps not even the chief, thing to say about the poem:

But how smooth, strong and elaborate it all is! What poetry! I can conceive that even Shakespeare after this would seem a little troubled, personal, hot and imperfect. I can conceive that this is the essence, of which almost all other poetry is the dilution.

This is, though, a purely *poetic* commendation, like that of Arnold—and Woolf knows that Milton cared about other things as much, or more. "Moreover, though there is nothing like Lady Macbeth's terror or Hamlet's cry, no pity or sympathy or intuition, the figures are majestic; in them is summed up much of what men thought of our place in the universe, of our duty to God, our religion."[6] The key point to make about this point is its tense: what men *thought*, not what men *think*. That Milton's theological concerns could be those of the twentieth century is scarcely conceivable to Woolf. A decade later she would write to her sister, Vanessa,

> I had a most shameful and distressing interview with poor dear Tom Eliot, who may be called dead to us all from this day forward. He has become an Anglo-Catholic, believes in God and immortality, and goes to church. I was really shocked. A corpse would seem to me more credible than he is. I mean, there's something obscene in a living person sitting by the fire and believing in God.[7]

Woolf was certainly not alone in this estrangement from religious belief. A few years later John Middleton Murry, in a

6. Woolf, *A Writer's Diary*, pp. 5–6.
7. Virginia Woolf, *A Change of Perspective: Letters of Virginia Woolf, III: 1923–1928*, ed. Nigel Nicolson (London: Hogarth Press, 1977, 1994), pp. 457–58.

book on Keats, warmly endorsed Keats's attitude towards Milton—"Life to him would be death to me"—and extends the critique, turning Macaulay's extravagant praise on its head: "On the moral and spiritual side I find it easy enough to place him: he is, simply, a bad man of a very particular kind, who is a bad man because he is so sublimely certain of being a good one." But that's a position Murry finds easy and trivial. The deeper puzzle involves "our dissatisfaction with Milton: which is that a poet so evidently great, in some valid sense of the word, should have so little intimate meaning for us. We cannot make him real. He does not, either in his great effects or his little ones, touch our depths."[8] Whatever he was for our ancestors he cannot be for us; there is a chasm between Milton and us that cannot be closed or crossed. Or so Murry thought.

Occasionally the matter of Milton's misogyny would be raised again, most notably by Robert Graves in his novel *Wife to Mr. Milton*, narrated by Milton's first wife, Marie Powell. At one point Milton—in his mid-thirties at this point, just beginning his career as a polemicist, and beginning to get to know young Marie, though he has already contracted with her father to marry her—is describing for Marie and a friend his idea (discussed in chapter 2 above) for a tragedy in the form of a morality play called *Adam Unparadised*. He explains— and here Graves closely paraphrases Milton's notebook— that, after the Fall, "Conscience, in a shape, follows after Adam and accuses him, and Justice cites Man to appear for God's examination." Marie, who has declared that she has no wish

---

8. John Middleton Murry, *Studies in Keats New and Old* (London: Oxford University Press, 1939 [1930]), pp. 110, 121–22.

to be thought "saucy," saucily intervenes to asks a question: "Does not Conscience also follow after Eve? Is she not also cited to appear?" But to this "Mr. Milton did not answer"; rather, he "raised his voice a little as if in warning against needless interruption" and continued his account. Marie is not so easily put off:

> "Pray tell me more of our mother Eve," said I. "Was she indeed untroubled by Conscience, and thereafter unrepentant, as seems from this account?"
>
> "The title of my drama," said Mr. Milton sternly, "is not *The Famous History of Adam and Eve*, as you would make it, but *Adam Unparadised*. Adam, being of the perfecter sex, is the protagonist, and Eve is but the incidental instrument, or accessory, of his crime against God."[9]

---

9. Robert Graves, *Wife of Mr. Milton: The Story of Marie Powell* (New York: Creative Age Press, 1944 [1943]), pp. 161–62. Those who recall Milton's description of Eve's "wanton ringlets" (IV.306) may be interested to note that Graves's Milton is initially compelled by Marie's hair:

> "Your hair delights my eye, pretty Child. Without doubt, Eve had tresses like yours."
>
> Then he said: "After I had seen you for the first time, your hair became an obsession of my mind: for it wreathed itself between my eye and what book soever I studied, though it might be the Holy Bible itself, coming with a gadding or serpentine motion until it choked the sense of my reading."

After further hermeneutical reflection, Milton decides that this fascination with Marie's tresses is a sign from God that he should marry her (p. 156).

Graves was also quite crtitical at times of Milton as a poet: In an essay called "John Milton Muddles Through" he takes apart Milton's early verse, finding "L'Allegro" "a dreadful muddle," discerns in other poems "careless repeating" and "padding," and declares of "Lycidas" that "No sensitive poet or critic can accept without a blush Milton's pastoral affectations."

Whether the younger Milton would have given such an answer cannot now be known; but, as we saw in the overview of
the poem in chapter 2, the Milton who wrote *Paradise Lost*
shows us an Eve afflicted by conscience before Adam is, and
who becomes the chief "instrument," not at all an incidental
one, by which Adam's conscience is awakened.

So far the twentieth-century responses to *Paradise Lost* are
what one might expect of responses to assured classics: a chorus of respect interspersed with occasional arias of protest. But
in the middle third of the twentieth century a greater debate
about Milton began, a debate that begins in one register but
then moved into another.

On that first register: Middleton Murry's sense that Milton
is great and yet somehow deficient—deficient *as a poet*, unable to cross the span of time, something that Shakespeare
does with ease—is the key claim. "Shakespeare baffles and
liberates; Milton is perspicuous and constricts." Ezra Pound's
comments on Milton (which span several decades) are bluntly
spiteful: "Milton is the worst sort of poison. He is a thorough-
going decadent in the worst sense of the term." That from
1915; in 1934 he lamented "The gross and utter stupidity and
obtuseness of Milton."[10] Pound's friend T. S. Eliot was more
circumspect, admitting in a 1936 essay that "that Milton is a
very great poet indeed," but immediately going on to add that
"it is something of a puzzle to decide in what his greatness
consists." He concludes by affirming that Milton has "done
damage to the English language from which it has not wholly

10. Ezra Pound, "The Renaissance," *Poetry* 5, no. 5 (Feb. 1915); and *ABC of Reading* (New York: New Directions, 1934), p. 103.

recovered." The chief problem, Eliot says, is not something intrinsic to Milton's verse but rather the consequence of his vast and overwhelming influence on later poets. (They'd have done better to be influenced by Dryden.)[11]

All of these criticisms are couched in strictly poetic, or more broadly intellectual terms: the critics speak of Milton's poetic "effects," of his poetic "decadence," of his poetic "influence." And yet something else keeps creeping in. Middleton Murry says that "Milton is perspicuous," but *about what* is he perspicuous? It's hard not to assume that it's his theology, the theology so closely connected to his "moral and spiritual side." Eliot insists that in responding to Milton he is overwhelmingly responding to sound—he thinks Milton, because of his blindness, is an excessively *aural* poet—but somewhat reluctantly acknowledges that he is also aware of what *Paradise Lost* is actually *about*: "So far as I perceive anything, it is a glimpse of a theology that I find in large part repellent, expressed through a mythology which would have better been left in the Book of Genesis, upon which Milton has not improved." Eliot does not explain what in Milton's theology strikes him as "repellent," though that would be interesting to learn since Milton's theology overlaps greatly with Eliot's own. But we can at least be confident that non-Christians like Pound and Middleton Murry (and for that matter Virginia Woolf) would be even more likely to find Milton's overwhelmingly Christian and biblical focus unpalatable.

So, no matter how consciously these critics try to distinguish their judgments of Milton's verse from their judgments

11. "Milton I," in T. S. Eliot, *On Poetry and Poets* (New York: Farrar, Straus and Giroux, 1957), pp. 156, 164.

of his religion, the separation doesn't hold. And thus, gradually, a debate about poetic merit and influence becomes a debate about the Christian views that Milton holds and defends. Thus the work of a seventeenth-century poet becomes the pretext for arguments about the ongoing validity (or lack thereof) of Christian belief. Milton criticism in the English-speaking world becomes a battlefield on which a kind of proxy war is fought: for lurking behind all these academic disputes are the massed opposing armies of the Believers and the Unbelievers. The War in Heaven is recapitulated as a War in Academic Publishing. Whether this is another case of "first as tragedy, then as farce" I leave for the reader to decide.

A key figure in this debate is a curious person named Charles Williams. He was a Londoner who never took a university degree, though he studied for a time at University College London. Later Williams became an influential editor at Oxford University Press, and, in his spare time, the author of several plays, much narrative verse, and several novels, "supernatural thrillers" they have often been called, the first of which happens to bear the title *War in Heaven*. He was close friends with both T. S. Eliot and C. S. Lewis—Lewis disliked and disapproved of Eliot, but they were fully agreed that Williams was a remarkable man—and W. H. Auden credited Williams with a major role in drawing him back to the Christianity of his childhood. Lewis had been corresponding with Williams for some years when Williams, along with other staff members of Oxford University Press, was evacuated to Oxford at the outset of World War II. Soon after his arrival he wrote an introduction to a collection of Milton's English poems, and that essay sets the terms for much of what would follow in the Miltonic War.

Williams begins his essay by writing, "We have been fortunate enough to live at a time when the reputation of John Milton has been seriously attacked." Fortunate? Yes: because the reputation of Milton had become too settled, he had become a "classic" in the Arnoldian sense. For the previous several decades Milton's reputation had been preserved and polished by "the orthodox party," by which Williams means not religious orthodoxy but critical orthodoxy: Milton had become (as it were) the *property* of a handful of meek custodians of poetic reputation.[12] Williams is therefore delighted that someone like Middleton Murry would straightforwardly call Milton "a bad man," and more delighted still that a critic as distinguished as T. S. Eliot would lament the influence of Milton over English verse. All of this tends to push us back to actual *reading*, a genuine encounter with Milton's poetry—and with his theology.

In this introduction Williams does not describe all of Milton's English verse. He focuses instead first on Milton's court masque *Comus*, then on *Paradise Lost, Paradise Regained*, and, briefly, the verse tragedy *Samson Agonistes*. He begins with *Comus* to call our attention to the fact that that poetic drama was written to defend what Williams calls "the Mystery of Chastity." Williams thinks that the attack on Milton's reputation just might force readers to ask themselves whether chastity is indeed a mystery, as opposed to a mere stricture or an irrational imposition. Williams wants us to attend to the shockingly bold claim that Milton is making in this work: that chastity is a beautiful thing and productive of great joy. "It may be true that we

---

12. Charles Williams, "Introduction," in *The English Poems of John Milton*, ed. H. C. Beeching (London: Oxford University Press, 1940), p. ix.

ourselves do not believe that to be so, but our disbelief is largely as habitual as our admiration of *Comus*. That is why it has been possible to admire *Comus* without any serious realization of the mystery of chastity."[13] The disruption to Milton's reputation just might, by breaking him out of his glass case, enable him to speak to us in a way that forces upon us a decision.

Williams then goes on to argue that chastity involves obedience to a particular moral law, but *Paradise Lost* is concerned with obedience in a more universal sense. He describes Satan as one who refuses obedience because he first refuses *dependence*. Williams limits his quotations in his short essay, but it seems clear which particular passages he has in mind. As we saw earlier, during his revolt against the Almighty the archangel denies that God created him: "We know no time when we were not as now; / Know none before us, self-begot, self-raised / By our own quickening power" (V.856–61). And it is precisely this belief that leads him later to say, when considering the possibility of turning back from his planned assault on God's newest creation, Humanity,

> O then at last relent: is there no place
> Left for repentance, none for pardon left?
> None left but by submission; and that word
> Disdain forbids me . . . (IV.79–81)

He must disdain a submission that refuses the very autonomy on which he had staked his initial rebellion. This contrast between those who think themselves self-created and those who delight in their "derivation" from another is, Williams says,

13. Williams, "Introduction," p. xii.

fundamental to Milton's verse. Near the end of his introduction he concludes

> Heaven is always unexpected to the self-loving spirit; he can never understand whence it derives, for he has self renounced all derivation, as do those who follow him. It was this great and fundamental fact of human existence which Milton very well understood; it was this which his genius exerted all his tenderness and all his sublimated sublimity to express.[14]

Note the character of this statement: Williams does not distance himself from Milton's claims about human nature and what brings us joy and what misery—as a professional academic critic might do, as a member of "the orthodox party" might do—but instead forthrightly declares his agreement with these claims: what Milton shows us in his contrast between obedience and disobedience is simply a "great and fundamental *fact* of human existence" (emphasis mine). Williams took the contemporary questions about the quality of Milton's verse as an opportunity to affirm his wholehearted agreement with Milton's theology; and in so doing he set the readerly cat among the scholarly pigeons.

———

At around the time that he wrote this introduction, Williams gave a lecture at Oxford on *Comus*—and therefore on chastity. His friend C. S. Lewis sat enraptured, and when he soon

14. Williams, "Introduction," p. x.

thereafter delivered his own lectures on Milton—lectures that would become one of the most influential and hotly contested books in the history of Milton studies—he began by dedicating the book to Williams and, in effect, crediting Williams with the inspiration for his own work. Here's what he wrote in the dedication of *A Preface to "Paradise Lost"*:

> You were a *vagus* thrown among us by the chance of war. The appropriate beauties of the Divinity School provided your background. There we elders heard (among other things) what he had long despaired of hearing—a lecture on *Comus* which placed its importance where the poet placed it—and watched "the yonge fresshe folkes, he or she," who filled the benches listening first with incredulity, then with toleration, and finally with delight, to something so strange and new in their experience as the praise of chastity. Reviewers, who have not had time to re-read Milton, have failed for the most part to digest your criticism of him; but it is a reasonable hope that of those who heard you in Oxford many will understand henceforward that when the old poets made some virtue their theme they were not teaching but adoring, and that what we take for the didactic is often the enchanted.[15]

It is this mutation of the didactic into the enchanted that Lewis hoped to achieve with his own work on Milton.

Thus Lewis makes his own assault on the "orthodox party," as represented by Professor Denis Saurat, a French scholar who lived and taught for many years in London and

---

15. Lewis, *A Preface to "Paradise Lost,"* p. v.

whose first book was titled *La pensée de Milton* (1920). Lewis declared,

> We must . . . turn a deaf ear to Professor Saurat when he invites us "to study what there is of lasting originality in Milton's thought and especially to disentangle from theological rubbish the permanent and human interest." . . . This is like asking us to study Hamlet after the "rubbish" of the revenge code has been removed, or centipedes when free of their irrelevant legs, or Gothic architecture without the pointed arches. Milton's thought, when purged of its theology, does not exist. Our plan must be very different to plunge right into the "rubbish," to see the world as if we believed it, and then, while we still hold that position in our imagination, to see what sort of a poem results.

So far, so scholarly—so "objective." An atheist studying Milton could make the same case. But Lewis immediately continues, "In order to take no unfair advantage I should warn the reader that I myself am a Christian, and that some (by no means all) of the things which the atheist reader must 'try to feel as if he believed' I actually, in cold prose, do believe."[16] And this, Lewis says, even the skeptical listener or reader should welcome, for would it not be helpful to have Lucretius explained to you by an actual Epicurean?

It is unlikely that Lewis's course of lectures, given in Wales in 1941, would have taken the form that they did if not for the example of Williams. Certainly this is what Lewis himself believed: "Apparently, the door of the prison was really unlocked

16. Lewis, *A Preface to "Paradise Lost,"* p. 65.

all the time; but it was only you who thought of trying the handle. Now we can all come out." Lewis had been writing Christian apologetics with his left hand, as it were, while doing reputable and in some cases quite influential scholarly work with his right hand, but Williams's lecture on *Comus* made him realize that the two endeavors could and should be joined, that it was possible to do a work of serious, scholarly literary criticism about *Paradise Lost* that provides an account of what Milton believed—and then goes still further, to affirm that what Milton believed is true. One can after all seek to justify the ways of Milton, and of the Christian God, to one's twentieth-century readers.[17]

Well; one may seek, but to succeed is another matter. Certainly he did not persuade that remarkable critic and writer William Empson. A native of Yorkshire, Empson studied mathematics at Cambridge, then added English, then abandoned mathematics (at which he was very good) for English (at which he was brilliant). He was granted a fellowship and commenced his poetic and academic career in Magdalene College—a short walk down Sidney Street from Christ's College, where Milton had studied—while living in quite extraordinary squalor. "The poet was alone when we entered," wrote one visitor; "lying in a welter of banana-skins, mathematical

---

17. It is tempting here to say a few words about Lewis's 1943 novel *Perelandra*, which imagines that God created sentient life, creatures made "in his own image" (Genesis 1:26), on Venus and installed them in a kind of garden, where they were then tempted—but did *not* fall. Lewis began this book soon after writing his lectures on *Paradise Lost*, but while writing about Milton may have stimulated his imagination, the deeper engagement in *Perelandra* is with the Genesis narrative itself and commentary on it by the Church Fathers, especially Augustine.

instruments, and abandoned pieces of paper, singing as he worked, and automatically writing with his left hand, he was patiently sucking some beer-stains out of the carpet."[18] Somehow he had managed to smuggle a woman into his rooms—why she did not immediately flee remains a mystery—then left condoms out where a college servant could see them. This offense against morals led an already suspicious master of Magdalene, Allen Ramsey, to end Empson's fellowship and banish him from the college.

Now Empson, at age twenty-three, embarked on a peripatetic and picaresque life, surviving for a time as a freelance writer in London—he published his first (and, it would prove, most lastingly famous) book, *Seven Types of Ambiguity*, in 1930. He then accepted a position as professor of English at Tokyo University of Literature and Science, where he taught until 1934, at which point he returned for a while to England before circling back to Asia, this time to teach in China, where he landed in the midst of the Sino-Japanese War. For two years he taught at several makeshift universities in conditions of real poverty and in the complete absence of books—he had to teach English literature from memory. Finally, in January of 1940, he made it back to England, only to discover that in his absence something disturbing had happened: "the revival of Christianity among literary critics," he wrote some years later, "has rather taken me by surprise."[19]

18. John Haffenden, *William Empson*, vol. 1, *Among the Mandarins* (Oxford: Oxford University Press, 2005), p. 249.

19. William Empson, *Milton's God*, rev. ed. (London: Chatto & Windus, 1965 [1961]), pp. 9–10. Empson did not publish this book until 1960, but throughout his

C. S. Lewis's *A Preface to "Paradise Lost"* caught his attention, in large part because Lewis "let in some needed fresh air" by bluntly stating, "Many of those who say they dislike Milton's God only mean that they dislike God."[20] Empson liked this forthrightness; it enabled more straightforward disputation: "'Dislike' is a question-begging term here. I think the traditional God of Christianity very wicked, and have done since I was at school, where nearly all my little playmates thought the same. I did not say this in my earlier literary criticism because I thought it could be taken for granted."

But apparently, and alas, it could no longer be taken for granted. "Having had ten years teaching in Japan and China, . . . I am still rather ill-adjusted to the change of atmosphere." Those Japanese and Chinese students who read *Paradise Lost* had, he felt, a perfectly reasonable reaction to it, which he sums up thus: "Well, if they worship such a monstrously wicked God as all that, no wonder that they themselves are so monstrously wicked as we have traditionally found them."[21] Empson did not expect, when he returned to England, to have

---

introduction he writes as if just returned from Asia. After spending the Second World War in England, he returned to China from 1947 to 1952, with visits to the United States; but at several points in *Milton's God* writes of "ten years teaching" as though it were one period from which he had recently returned. I expect that, being an attentive and wide-ranging reader, he started seeing the rise of what he called scholarly "Neo-Christians" soon after his resettling in England in 1940, even though he apparently did not see the movement as "widespread" until 1952 (see p. 230).

20. Lewis, *A Preface to "Paradise Lost,"* p. 130.

21. If indeed there were no books for these students, and Empson had to teach them *Paradise Lost* from his own memory, that just might account for some of the hostility they developed towards Milton's God. Oh, to have been a fly on the wall as Empson ventriloquized Milton.

to speak of these matters, but since it had become after all necessary, he was grateful to Lewis for openly confessing his adherence to Christianity, and to the Christianity expressed through the story of *Paradise Lost*. This made it possible for Empson to do something that otherwise he would have thought both irrelevant and impolite: to declare his deep-seated and passionate hatred of the Christian God—and of (the title of the book he eventually wrote) *Milton's God*.[22] The first volume of John Haffenden's massive biography of Empson is subtitled *Among the Mandarins*; the second, quite rightly, is subtitled *Against the Christians*. And *Paradise Lost* is always central to Empson's thinking about the shocking and baffling *wrongness* of Christian belief.

Like many readers before and since, Empson was disgusted by the Father portrayed in *Paradise Lost*. And he was exasperated by Christian readers who shared that disgust but tried to deal with it by distinguishing Milton's God from the God of the Bible—by attributing their discomfort to some supposed heresy of Milton's. It was, he thought, shamefully evasive action, for the single most offensive aspect of the God of *Paradise Lost*—the idea that the divine wrath is somehow "satisfied" by the blood-sacrifice of God's own Son—is the single most essential idea of traditional Christianity. Thus Empson's admiration of Lewis, who in saying that "those who say they

22. Perhaps surprisingly, Empson and Lewis got along very well indeed. Though they met in person rarely, they exchanged friendly letters, and each of them reviewed the other's work positively. In an interview in 1969, six years after Lewis's death, Empson said, "I wish I had seen more of C. S. Lewis. You think people aren't going to die and then they do." John Haffenden, *William Empson*, vol. 2, *Against the Christians* (Oxford: Oxford University Press, 2006), p. 399.

dislike Milton's God only mean that they dislike God" had firmly grasped the nettle. Opposition to Milton's God *is* opposition to the Christian God, for they are one and the same, says Lewis. This is precisely the issue to be debated, says Empson. An honest critic must acknowledge that one's response to *Paradise Lost* is to some degree linked to one's view of Christianity.

And what was Empson's view of *Paradise Lost*? Perhaps his most compelling and provocative summation of his (admittedly complex) view is this:

> The poem is not good in spite of but especially because of its moral confusions, which ought to be clear in your mind when you are feeling its power. I think it horrible and wonderful; I regard it as like Aztec or Benin sculpture, or to come nearer home the novels of Kafka, and am rather suspicious of any critic who claims not to feel anything so obvious.[23]

23. Empson, *Milton's God*, p. 13. In 1959, when asked to provide a description of his forthcoming book, Empson offered this:

Professor Empson's new book surveys the main arguments of the controversy about *Paradise Lost* which has been so lively for thirty years, and claims to show that the poem feels much better if the objections to it are accepted and taken seriously; because, though thought of as literary, they are at bottom theological. The poem is wonderful because it is an awful warning, not against eating the apple but against worshipping that God; it is like Aztec or Benin sculpture, or the novels of Kafka, which raise our spirits by the same method of letting us experience a mode of life which our consciences or good sense forbid us to follow. The decision of Empson is against any form of Christianity, in the last chapter of the book; but he recognises that most modern Christians would also be strongly against Milton's God. The pressure of their Communist opponents, he considers, is very likely to make them start burning people alive again, though it is the

Why "horrible" is, I hope, obvious; but why "wonderful"? Wonderful because of the matchless intelligence and poetic resourcefulness with which Milton grasps the same nettle that Lewis grasped.

To be sure, in grasping that nettle Milton determines "To justify the ways of God to man," to *defend* God—to make him more appealing than he might otherwise seem to be. Empson acknowledges this goal and grants that Milton is to some degree successful; those Christian readers who think Milton's God morally inferior to the God *they* worship, Empson believes, have it precisely backwards. Milton

> does succeed in making [God] noticeably less wicked than the traditional Christian one; though, after all his efforts, owing to his loyalty to the sacred text and the penetration with which he makes its story real to us, his modern critics still feel, in a puzzled way, that there is something badly wrong about it all. That this searching goes on in *Paradise Lost*, I submit, is the chief source of its fascination and poignancy.[24]

*Poignancy* may seem an odd word here, but it's well chosen: Empson is moved, *touched* by the scene laid out before him, in which a man less wicked than the religion he professes strives, with astonishing intelligence and artistic power, to

_____

last thing they intend; so that the effort of reconsidering Milton's God, who makes the poem so good just because he is so sickeningly bad, is a basic one of the European mind.

William Empson, *Selected Letters of William Empson*, ed. John Haffenden (Oxford: Oxford University Press, 2006), p. 294.

24. Empson, *Milton's God*, p. 11.

make that religion seem less wicked than it is. It is for Empson a unique kind of poetic greatness.

And then, having established the greatness, he takes up the sadly necessary task of reminding his readers what grotesque nonsense Christianity is. The final chapter of *Milton's God* is called "Christianity," and it scarcely mentions Milton; instead, Empson embarks on an anthropological, historical, and moral critique of the only one of the world's great religions "which dragged back the Neolithic craving for human sacrifice into its basic structure."[25]

———

Late in his life, Empson wrote to a friend, "The monstrous Fish I have heard in action; I happened to visit Princeton when he was holding a kind of discussion group there, and was kindly invited to join it."[26] Who or what was this "monstrous Fish"? It was Stanley Fish, then a professor at Johns Hopkins, the author of *Surprised by Sin: The Reader in "Paradise Lost"* (1967), a witty and brilliant attempt to explain, and to transcend, the argument between Lewis and Empson by declaring that both were right—and wrong. Indeed, Fish contends that the entire history of responses to *Paradise Lost*—those by Addison and Percy Shelley, by Virginia Woolf and Charles Williams, by Lewis and Empson—are artifacts of the poem itself.

The poem demands each of these readings and to leave any of them out would manifest a gross insensitivity to the poem's

25. Empson, *Milton's God*, p. 241.
26. Empson, *Selected Letters*, p. 666.

rhetorical strategies and practices. I make a point of saying the *poem's* strategies and practices rather than *Milton's* because that is the primary way Fish articulates his argument—primary, not only: though he is often accused of eliminating the author (Empson makes that accusation in the letter I quote above), in fact he often refers to what Milton is thinking and doing. But his emphasis is on the poem as a thing that acts.

This description makes Fish sound like a New Critic, or one of the Modernist poets who inspired the New Criticism. William Carlos Williams, for instance, wrote that "A poem is a small (or large) machine made of words."[27] But what kind of machine is a poem like *Paradise Lost*? The relevant example here comes not from poetry or literary criticism but from the behaviorism of B. F. Skinner. On Fish's account, *Paradise Lost* is a Skinner box—an operant conditioning chamber—made of words. It is an environment in which certain stimuli are imposed upon a reader, and the responses to those stimuli registered and evaluated. The poem is a verbal structure, composed of verbal patterns, that reliably generate revulsion and admiration, rebellion and worship. The entire future history of the reading of *Paradise Lost* is contained within the machine itself. It is a uniquely powerful stimulus-response device.

A useful example—though one not cited by Fish himself[28]—comes early in the poem, when the rebel angels, thrown down

27. From the introduction to his 1944 collection of poems, *The Wedge*. That introduction has been widely republished elsewhere, for instance here: https://www.poetryfoundation.org/articles/69410/introduction-to-the-wedge.

28. It has struck me since I first read *Surprised by Sin*, some forty years ago, that the passage I present here is a perfect illustration of his argument; but he does not use it in either *Surprised by Sin* or his later book *How Milton Works*. He mentions

into the pit of Hell, decide to build for themselves a city, which Milton calls Pandemonium. The architect and builders get to work, and then when they're done invite the other rebels to inspect their new residence. Milton goes on for some time about the magnificence of the structures, and then offers us this account:

> The hasty multitude
> Admiring entered, and the work some praise
> And some the architect: his hand was known
> In heaven by many a towered structure high,
> Where sceptred angels held their residence,
> And sat as princes, whom the supreme king
> Exalted to such power, and gave to rule,
> Each in his hierarchy, the orders bright.
> Nor was his name unheard or unadored
> In ancient Greece; and in Ausonian land
> Men called him Mulciber; and how he fell
> From heaven, they fabled, thrown by angry Jove
> Sheer o'er the crystal battlements; from morn
> To noon he fell, from noon to dewy eve,
> A summer's day; and with the setting sun
> Dropped from the zenith like a falling star,
> On Lemnos the Aegaean isle: thus they relate,
> Erring; for he with this rebellious rout
> Fell along before; nor aught availed him now

the passage in a general way a couple of times, but not the "gotcha" that comes at the end of the long sentence—except in a short piece he wrote for the *New York Times* website in 2008, "Happy Birthday, Milton." I can't resist performing my own Fishian reading here.

To have built in heaven high towers; nor did he scape
By all his engines, but was headlong sent
With his industrious crew to build in hell. (I.730–51)

This is one of the most magnificent passages in the entire poem: there can be few lines in English verse more glorious than "from morn / To noon he fell, from noon to dewy eve, / A summer's day; and with the setting sun / Dropped from the zenith like a falling star"—but, Milton insists, it's all a lie. He has already indicated as much by beginning his account of the Greek myth of Hephaestus (or Mulciber, or Vulcan) with the word *fabled*, but then come those irresistibly gorgeous lines that catch us up—Eliot's claim that Milton's blindness made him too purely aural could scarcely survive an encounter with the *visual* splendor of this passage—so that we have to be pulled up short by a zinger of an enjambment: "Thus they relate, / Erring."

*Erring.* It's all a tale, a fable that arises largely from forgetting—for *something* of the real story has survived in the image of a God falling from a great high place to something far, far lower, but not the *essential* thing: the moral and spiritual ugliness of his rebellion against a just and loving God. If we are moved by this description of Hephaestus's fall, is that simply because the verse is so lovely? Or are we also inclined towards an account that would transform the demon into a mistreated god, a helpless victim of *Zeus Brontaios*, Zeus the Thunderer, an unreasonably and unpredictably angry king of the gods—king, not creator, for he is made of the same stuff as Hephaestus. If we are drawn to this aestheticizing and relativizing of the story, is that not because we are already predisposed to sympathy with Satan's account of, not what he *did*, he would say, but what *has befallen* him? Already in his first speech he has said, "What matter where, if I be still the same, / And what I should be, all but less than he / Whom thunder hath made greater?" (I.256–58)

On Fish's account, then, the act of reading *Paradise Lost* is an ongoing moral and spiritual education. The poem constantly invites responses which it then critiques. The intense hatred of Shelley, the horror of Empson, the bored puzzlement of Woolf, are responses anticipated in the poem, indeed *drawn out by* the poem, and drawn out in such a way as to make them available for inspection. As Fish puts it, "The comment of the epic voice unsettles the reader, who sees in it at least a partial challenge to his own assessment of the speech"[29]—whatever speech that might be, most probably one made by Satan. *This is how you feel*, the poem whispers to us; *but is this how you* want *to feel? What within you generates this feeling? Are you pleased with yourself for feeling this way—or distressed?* In their various ways, Addison, and the Godwins and the Shelleys, and Woolf, and Williams and Lewis, and Empson all hear and respond to this whisper. Only those who condescendingly name *Paradise Lost* an "English classic" refuse the invitation altogether. They make sure that they don't hear a sound.

In *Tetrachordon*, one of his tracts on divorce, Milton describes the teaching of Jesus as "not so much a teaching as an intangling," and this phrase is central to Fish: it provides the title both of the first chapter and of the first section of the final chapter of *Surprised by Sin*. The poem subjects us to a kind of

29. Stanley Fish, *Surprised by Sin: The Reader in "Paradise Lost"* (Berkeley: University of California Press, 1965), p. 5.

psychoanalysis, with the understanding that *psyche* should indicate "soul" as well as "mind." One must become "intangled" in perplexities by reading the poem, one must cease to coincide with oneself. Almost immediately after making that remark on "intangling," Milton adds that "it is a general precept, not only of Christ, but of all other Sages, not to instruct the unworthy and the conceited who love tradition more than truth, but to perplex and stumble them purposely with contrived obscurities."[30] The question, then, is whether one holds firm to the wrong notions that lead to perplexity, or rises above them to a better, truer understanding of oneself, of the world, of God. "The monstrous Fish" agrees with Empson that *Paradise Lost* is beset by "confusions"—but suggests that those confusions are located not in the poem but rather in the psyche of its reader.

In 1996 Stanley Fish published an essay in the magazine *First Things*, a magazine put out by the Institute on Religion and Public Life, which describes itself as "an interreligious, nonpartisan research and education institute whose purpose is to advance a religiously informed public philosophy for the ordering of society," but which was at the time closely associated, through its founding editor Father Richard John Neuhaus, with neoconservatism. This was not the sort of venue one might expect a prominent literary critic and theorist to publish in. Fish's essay was called "Why We Can't All Just Get Along."[31]

---

30. *Complete Prose Works of John Milton*, vol. 2, *1643–1648*, ed. Ernest Sirluck (New Haven: Yale University Press, 1959), pp. 642–43.

31. Stanley Fish, "Why We Can't All Just Get Along," *First Things*, February 1996. Every reader of the magazine at that time would have gotten the reference. In

We can't all just get along, Fish says, because we understand the world in fundamentally different ways, indeed in incommensurable ways. And he presses religious believers—whether he is or is not one of them he does not say—to ask themselves what price they are willing to pay to "get along" with people whose understanding of the world cannot be reconciled with their own. He shakes his head wryly at religious believers who ask the culturally dominant "liberal proceduralists"—people who understand our social order as one which suspends or brackets metaphysical commitments and asks us, whatever our metaphysics or lack thereof, to agree to follow common procedures for securing peace—to allow them "a seat at the table." Says Fish, "If you persuade liberalism that its dismissive marginalizing of religious discourse is a violation of its own chief principle, all you will gain is the right to sit down at liberalism's table where before you were denied an invitation; but it will still be *liberalism's* table that you are sitting at, and the etiquette of the conversation will still be hers."

It is a fascinating argument in many respects, but its chief interest for our purposes here is how Fish begins the essay: by arguing with William Empson about *Paradise Lost.*

Whenever I teach *Paradise Lost*, the hardest thing to get across is that God is God. Students invariably (one is

---

March of 1991 a Black man named Rodney King was severely beaten by Los Angeles police officers, who were eventually arrested and charged with assault and excessive use of force. To almost everyone's surprise, indeed, shock, in April of 1992 they are all acquitted. The decision sparked riots through the city of Los Angeles, and Rodney King himself eventually appeared on television to plead for an end to the riots: "I just want to say—you know—can we, can we all get along? Can we, can we get along?"

tempted to say "naturally") fall in with the view declared by William Empson in *Milton's God* when he says that "all the characters are on trial in any civilized narrative." In Milton's narrative, of course, God is a central character, and the entire story gets going, Empson observes, when Satan "doubts his credentials." Empson analogizes the situation to that "of a Professor doubting the credentials of his Vice-Chancellor," and remarks with some sarcasm that "such a man would not be pursued with infinite malignity into eternal torture, but given evidence which put the credentials beyond doubt."

Fish thinks that Empson—as much of a liberal proceduralist as Fish's students—simply misunderstands what is at stake in the poem, what challenge the poem is making to us. (One of the biggest problems proceduralists have is seeing that there is any alternative to proceduralism.) According to Empson, the loyal angel Abdiel tells Satan and his fellow rebels "that God should be obeyed because he is good";[32] but, Fish points out, that's not what Abdiel says. Rather, his argument is this:

"Shalt thou give law to God, shalt thou dispute
With him the points of liberty, who made
Thee what thou art?" (V.822–24)

Thus: Not because God is *good* but because God is *God* should he be obeyed. For Abdiel, Fish says, "even to put God to such an evidentiary test would be a category mistake—how can you give a grade to the agent whose person defines and embodies value?—that would constitute the gravest of sins,

32. Empson, *Milton's God*, p. 94.

whether one calls it impiety ('Cease . . . this impious rage'), self-worship, or simply pride."[33]

In his long book *How Milton Works*, which appeared five years after his *First Things* essay, Fish describes a series of temptations faced by the reader of Milton: "the temptation to action," "the temptation of speech," "the temptation of plot," "the temptation of understanding," "the temptation of intelligibility," and finally, "the temptation of history and politics." All of these are temptations because they take the Christian story as a means to an end. If we read the story aright then we will know how to act, or we will understand, or we will be able to comprehend history and exercise political judgment. All such ideas distract us from what Fish believes to have been the only point that Milton really wishes to make: that "God is God." Fish uses this phrase over and over again, describing our endlessly imaginative ways of avoiding the acknowledgment that God is the maker and sustainer of all things, the one beyond all understanding, the one whose will is impossible to resist.

Fish insists that we cannot think of God in a way that does not demote him. To think of him as the sovereign over all things is almost invariably to think of him as merely one of those things, even if the most powerful. To think of there being some conflict or contest between God and Satan is to succumb to the "temptation of plot," which is to say, the temptation of redescribing God as a character in a story whose resolution is (if only for a time) in doubt. "Everything that many readers find interesting in Milton's work—crises, conflicts, competing values, once and for all dramatic moments—proceeds from error

33. Fish, "Why We Can't All Just Get Along."

and is finally unreal."[34] Error—deviation from the true path, departure from the saving center—is history, and its attractions are therefore as "natural" as they are fatal to entry into true life. What true life requires is "a new self, a self reborn outside of history, or more precisely a self that is born by virtue of being parted from history . . . Newborn into a historical reality."

The last full chapter of *How Milton Works* is titled "On Other Surety None," and that phrase also concludes the chapter.[35] It comes from Raphael's warning to Adam in Book V:

> Myself and all the angelic host that stand
> In sight of God enthroned, our happy state
> Hold, as you yours, while our obedience holds;
> On other surety none; freely we serve,
> Because we freely love, as in our will
> To love or not; in this we stand or fall. . . . (V.535–40)

There is no "surety," no guarantee, other than obedience, and obedience arises from faith, and faith will always be precisely that, *faith* rather than demonstrated conviction.[36] For Fish, this point is absolutely central to Milton's thought,

34. Stanley Fish, *How Milton Works* (Cambridge: Harvard University Press, 2001), p. 572.

35. Fish, *How Milton Works*, p. 559.

36. Fish, *How Milton Works*, p. 28: "To those in whose breast it lodges, the holy is everywhere evident as the first principle of both seeing and doing. If you regard the world as God's book before you ever take a particular look at it, any look you take will reveal, even as it generates, traces of his presence. If, on the other hand, the reality and omnipresence of God is not a basic premise of your consciousness, nothing you see will point to it and no amount of evidence will add up to it."

especially as it is manifested in *Paradise Lost*, but it is also the point that we readers most earnestly want to reject. That is, we want to assimilate the story to categories we are familiar with and know how to deploy. The radical, inescapable choice between absolute faith and equally absolute unbelief, neither of which we ever want to accept *as* absolute, is just what Milton wants to present us with and just what, in Fish's view, all parties to this proxy war wish to avoid.

# 6

# New Visions, New Media

REFERENCES AND allusions—I'm a literary critic, I *love* references and allusions. For people like me, finding an allusion to a literary work in a movie is like finding a lucky penny. Here's one:

In Woody Allen's movie *Deconstructing Harry* (1997), Allen plays a writer named Harry Block. Late in the film he's asked what he plans to write next and he says he's working on a story about a man whose beloved is kidnapped by the Devil. So the man takes the elevator down into Hell to try to rescue her. He meets the Devil (Billy Crystal), who says, "I've been offered a lot of jobs in your world, but, uh, why should I be an employee? Here I'm my own boss, you know, and I'm free." And Harry replies, "Better to rule down here than serve in heaven, right? That's Milton, I think."

Oh, and here's another, a bigger one, and from the same year: In *Devil's Advocate*, Keanu Reeves plays Kevin Lomax, a young lawyer who moves to New York City to work for an old, more experienced lawyer (Al Pacino), who turns out to be the Devil himself. But what's his human name? Why, John Milton. A nice turn. *Of* the Devil's party? He *is* the Devil's party. And when Milton denounces God as a "sadist" and an "absentee landlord," Kevin uses the same line as Harry Block but manages to get the quotation right: "Better to reign in Hell than serve in Heaven, is that it?"

As I say, we allusion-mongers love these quotes and echoes, and we love to think them important. But they aren't, not really. They're fun, but not important, because there's no genuine engagement with Milton here, with his characters or his story. Neither Billy Crystal's comically urbane Satan nor Al Pacino's scenery-chewing histrionic one have anything at all to do with the Satan of *Paradise Lost*. He's only useful to provide a line or two to please the people who happened to be paying attention in English literature class.

I wonder whether any attempt to film *Paradise Lost* itself will ever happen. The prospect has been mooted many times, and apparently a version helmed by Australian director Alex Proyas, and starring Bradley Cooper as Satan, came very close to being made in the early 2010s, but was scrapped—and scrapped because the necessary special effects would have been too expensive.[1] But even if it had been made, how much of Milton's story, and of the Bible's story, would have survived?

In a 1978 letter to the *New York Review of Books*, Empson imagined a period "when practically every homestead right across America was going to contain a copy of *Paradise Lost* as well as the King James Bible," thereby grossly overestimating the literary sophistication, and interest, of Americans.[2] Milton's

---

1. So says this story: https://deadline.com/2012/02/paradise-lost-scrapped-by -legendary-pictures-228682/.

2. Empson, *Selected Letters*, p. 643.

poem was rarely a major source of spiritual consolation for families huddled in little houses on the prairie—their hymnals better met that need—but the King James Bible was certainly a part of every house's furniture, and familiarity with its contents was pretty common as well, and not just in America. A hundred years ago, even Virginia Woolf, an unbeliever raised in an unbelieving household, was significantly more biblically and theologically literate than many Christians today. In a diary entry from 1929, she recalled a period (when she was fifteen or sixteen) when she wrote "a long picturesque essay upon the Christian religion, I think; called *Religio Laici*, I believe, proving that man has need of a God; but the God was described in process of change."[3] Moreover, the third essay of her late book *Three Guineas* (1938) contains a thorough critique of St. Paul's views of women which reveals not only her detailed knowledge of the New Testament but also the expectation that her readers will be equally familiar with those texts.

The world in which a lifelong agnostic or atheist could have or expect such knowledge has passed far away. And with declining religious adherence and biblical literacy, how could *Paradise Lost*, for the general public, amount to much more than a handful of sharp phrases? "Better to reign in Hell than serve in Heaven," is one, as we have seen, and how many more? "Justify the ways of God to man," perhaps; certainly "The mind is its own place, and in itself / Can make a heaven of hell, a hell of heaven" (I.254–55)—though this is often accepted as a Wise Saying rather than the catastrophic error that, in the

3. Woolf, *A Writer's Diary*, p. 147.

FIGURE 7. The video game *Paradise Lost*,
by PolyAmorous Games (2021).

poem, it quickly proves to be.[4] There are several songs called
"The Mind Is Its Own Place," none of which, as far as I can tell,
owes anything at all to Milton.

The most evocative phrase of all is, of course, the title itself,
which still appears in a thousand guises. A book about the destruction of the largely Greek-speaking Turkish city of Smyrna
is called *Paradise Lost: Smyrna 1922*, and its author is one Giles
Milton. One wonders how many copies of the book have been
sold to people who asked bookstore clerks for "Milton's *Paradise Lost*." Milton's epic gives its name to a video game—more

---

4. As noted in chapter 4, Satan discovers his error when he comes to earth:

> Me miserable! which way shall I fly
> Infinite wrath, and infinite despair?
> Which way I fly is hell; myself am hell;
> And in the lowest deep a lower deep
> Still threatening to devour me opens wide,
> To which the hell I suffer seems a heaven. (IV.73–78)

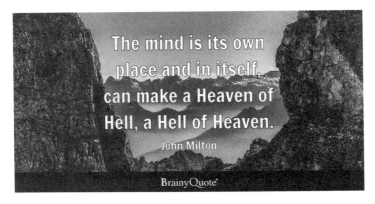

FIGURE 8. From the website BrainyQuote (https://www
.brainyquote.com/quotes/john_milton_110201).

than one video game, in fact—and (in 2003) a Wonder Woman
comic book,[5] which was followed the next year by a sequel
called *Paradise Found.*[6] A similar revising of the title had been
done many years before by John Mortimer, in a novel called
*Paradise Postponed* (1985); this story of a rising working-class
Conservative politician named Leslie Titmuss also yielded a
sequel, *Titmuss Regained* (1990). The jokes write themselves.

One could go on with this kind of thing, but the point
is that these echoes of Milton's title do not in any way suggest
the cultural currency of the poem, or even of the biblical story
that undergirds it. They are nearly free-floating signifiers: they
bear at most a vague penumbra of exile and guilt.

5. See https://www.dc.com/graphic-novels/wonder-woman-1987/wonder
-woman-paradise-lost.

6. See https://www.dc.com/graphic-novels/wonder-woman-1987/wonder
-woman-paradise-found.

More interesting, though also more difficult to talk meaningfully about, are the many translations of *Paradise Lost* that have appeared in the twentieth and twenty-first centuries. As Angelica Duran and Islam Issa note in the introduction to a collection of essays on *Milton in Translation*, "Recent scholarship has scarcely taken note that Milton's works have been translated into more languages in the last three decades at the turn of the twenty-first century than in the preceding three centuries."[7] For a gathering of scholarly essays, *Milton in Translation* is remarkable for its dramatic twists. Especially noteworthy is the story of Milovan Djilas, the Montenegran Communist leader who helped Josip Broz Tito create the Partisan army in Yugoslavia, turned against Tito for what he believed to be corruption, was thrown into prison, and devoted much of his imprisonment to translating *Paradise Lost*. Forbidden pen and paper, he managed to acquire a small pencil that he hid in an orange, and wrote with it on toilet paper. The determination of Zhu Weizhi to complete his own translation during the many dislocations and terrors of China's Cultural Revolution is almost as remarkable.

It would be rash of me to make any sort of definitive statement here, since the cultural contexts are often little known and sometimes wholly unknown to me, but if there are specific motives for these translations of Milton's epic—aside from wanting to make an acknowledged classic of world literature—they *seem*

7. Angelica Duran, Islam Issa, and Jonathan R. Olson, eds., *Milton in Translation* (Oxford: Oxford University Press, 2017), p. 4. Duran and Issa have also collaborated to edit a volume—highly relevant to this chapter—that, as I write, has not yet been published: *Milton across Borders and Media* (Oxford: Oxford University Press, 2024).

to orbit the concepts of rebellion, dissent, punishment. This is not to say that the recent translators of *Paradise Lost* are of the Devil's party—they may or may not be; I would love to know— but only that they are concerned with the things that also concern Satan and his fellow rebels. If any substantially theological or religious concerns undergird these translations, I cannot discern them. As Thomas N. Corns notes in a perceptive essay on the global reputation of Milton, one can in this respect contrast *Paradise Lost* to Bunyan's *The Pilgrim's Progress*, which has been translated into many of the world's languages precisely as an aid to Christian evangelism. However sincere Milton's desire to "justify the ways of God to Man," he did not write a poem that readily lends itself to the work of religious conversion.[8]

About *adaptation* as distinct from *translation* there may be more to be said. Earlier in the book I noted Dryden's idea that *Paradise Lost* could take dramatic form, and while his version in the event was not staged, his idea is a deeply perceptive and generative one. Milton's poem, with its combination of formal address, vaunting declamation, and overwhelming emotion, cries out for dramatic rendering: more specifically, it is—we can now see, in the aftermath of Mozart and Wagner and Verdi—spectacularly *operatic*.

A Verdi setting of *Paradise Lost*—what a beautiful dream. And yet the poem may be rather too angular and intellectually

8. Thomas N. Corns, "Milton's Global Reach," in *Milton in Translation*, p. 24. All this duly noted, Corns adds, "Just as Bunyan's engaging and accessible allegory finds a role in the British imperial experience, so Milton had a sort of high-culture equivalent in the work particularly of nonconformist missionaries, both British and US, to China" (p. 29).

dense for the musical resources of nineteenth-century operatic style to cope with—not that there weren't attempts, in several countries and languages. In German, Anton Rubenstein's *Das Verlorene Paradies* (1875); in French, Theodore Du Bois's *Le Paradis Perdu* (1878); in Italian, Marco Enrico Bossi's *Il Paradiso Perduto* (1903). There was even, in 1804, an *opéra comique* in French, composed by by an Italian named Gaspare Spontini, called *Milton*. It gives Milton a daughter, Emma, who captures the affections of Sir William Davenant—a real poet and playwright, often rumored over the years to be the illegitimate son of William Shakespeare, though that, perhaps unfortunately, does not feature in the opera. Davenant assumes a disguise, then with the assistance of a Quaker named Godwin saves Milton from political persecution, and finally wins the hand of fair Emma. *Comique* indeed, and all in one act.

A serious—and successful—attempt to set *Paradise Lost* to music had to wait until 1978, which is when Krzysztof Penderecki's opera had its premiere. Penderecki was born in 1933 in Poland, and had a long and distinguished career as a composer, one which began very much within the avant-garde—and a dark version of it, too. As Alex Ross has written, after World War II "composers took up what might be called catastrophe style with a vengeance, history having justified their instinctive attraction to the dreadful and the dire. Krzysztof Penderecki one-upped his colleagues by producing, within one decade, *Threnody for the Victims of Hiroshima* and *Dies Irae (Auschwitz Oratorio).*"[9] But around the time of that latter

9. Alex Ross, *The Rest Is Noise: Listening to the Twentieth Century* (New York: Picador, 2007), p. 484.

work (1967) his music took a turn—towards the religious. He was still interested in the tragic events of history, but was increasingly interested in giving those events a supernatural coloration, as in his first opera, *The Devils of Loudun* (1969), based on Aldous Huxley's 1952 book of the same title, about possible demonic possession in a seventeenth-century convent. He had already by this point written a *St. Luke Passion* (1966), and was gradually shifting his musical style from the radically exploratory to something often called neo-Romanticism—a move that outraged many who had seen him as one of the most prominent and promising exponents of new music.

Still, the leadership of the Lyric Opera of Chicago had to have been surprised and bemused, when, having accepted a commission to write something for a celebration of the American bicentennial, Penderecki turned in (two years late) an opera based on *Paradise Lost*. *Opera*, however, is not the word that Penderecki chose to describe his work: he called it a *sacra rappresentazione*, a "sacred performance," thereby associating himself with a musical genre of the Italian Renaissance. Each *sacra rappresentazione* would tell, in words and music, the story of a biblical character or a saint. For instance, a Florentine writer named Antonia Tanini Pulci—surely one of the few women involved in this genre—wrote works about Joseph the patriarch and Saint Francis, plus (circa 1490) one called *Destruzione di Saul e il pianto di Davit* ("The Destruction of Saul and the Weeping of David"). Even Lorenzo da Medici (Lorenzo il Magnifico) got into the act, writing in his native Tuscan dialect a *Sacra rappresentazione dei santi Giovanni e Paolo*—Saints John and Paul. Such *rappresentazioni* were sometimes merely read in private rather than set to music and

NEW VISIONS, NEW MEDIA    167

performed publicly, but Penderecki is clearly interested in the poetic and musical aspects of the genre.

For his attempt to revive this ancient dramatic genre, Penderecki chose as his librettist the English playwright Christopher Fry—and an excellent choice it is. Fry is almost completely forgotten now, and his star had already dimmed by the time Penderecki sought him out, but twenty-five years earlier he had been a major force in British theater: at one point he had three plays at once running in London's West End, and in 1950 he was featured on the cover of *Time*. He accompanied T. S. Eliot in an attempt to revive verse drama; while the attempt seemed for a while to flourish, it was soon overwhelmed by more colloquial and rough-hewn styles. Still, if in the mid-1970s one wanted someone to produce a libretto based on *Paradise Lost*, it would be difficult to think of a better candidate than Fry.

To his great credit, Fry realized that all the words one required for operatic singing—aria and recitative alike—were to be found present and awaiting employment in Milton's poem. What was required was largely selection and arrangement. So, for instance, Fry begins with close, if reduced, paraphrase of the opening of Milton's third book. Here are the first lines of Book III:

Hail holy light, offspring of heaven first-born,
Or of the eternal co-eternal beam
May I express thee unblamed?

And here are the first lines of Fry's libretto, to be sung by Milton:

Hail, holy light!
Before the Sun, before the Heavens thou wert.

May I express Thee?
But thou revisitest not these eyes
That roll in vain to find thy piercing ray.
Thus with the year
Seasons return, but not to me returns
Day, or the sweet approach of Eve or Morn.
Or Summer's Rose, or human face divine.
Shine inward.
There plant eyes, that I may see,
And tell of things invisible to mortal sight.[10]

Fry has selected certain lines from later in Milton's address to "holy light," lines that refer to his blindness:

> . . . thee I revisit safe,
> And feel thy sovereign vital lamp; but thou
> Revisit'st not these eyes, that roll in vain
> To find thy piercing ray, and find no dawn . . . (III.21–24)

And:

> Thus with the year
> Seasons return, but not to me returns
> Day, or the sweet approach of even or morn,
> Or sight of vernal bloom, or summer's rose,
> Or flocks, or herds, or human face divine;
> But cloud instead, and ever-during dark
> Surrounds me, from the cheerful ways of men
> Cut off, and for the book of knowledge fair

10. Fry's libretto for Krzysztof Penderecki, *Paradise Lost: Rappresentazione* (Mainz: Schott, 1978), p. 5.

Presented with a universal blank
Of nature's works to me expunged and razed,
And wisdom at one entrance quite shut out.
(III.40–50)

This is Fry's method throughout: selection, reduction, weaving. Occasionally he complicates the narrative, as when he creates in the opening scene a flash-forward to the events following the Fall: the first words Adam sings in the opera are "O fleeting joys of Paradise / Dear bought with lasting woes," an exact quotation of X.741–42.

But Fry adds, also in act I, a somewhat disconcerting chorus of children playing the animals that Adam names:[11] for instance, Adam dramatically sings, "Thou Horse," and the boisterous choral Horse replies, "Thou Horse, Thou Horse / Neigh, Neigh."[12] (This event is mentioned only briefly by Milton [VIII.349–55], so Fry is doing a rare expansion here.) Penderecki sets this to playful music, tonal if not always harmonious, that sometimes features tripping pizzicato strings, sometimes rather blustery horns, sometimes brisk drums. The music is not *altogether* happy, perhaps because Adam is about to confess that the beasts do not offer him any genuine companionship, but its carnival atmosphere is certainly cheerful in comparison to what it succeeds: a depiction of Satan's passage through Chaos on his way

11. Genesis 2:19–20: "And out of the ground the Lord God formed every beast of the field, and every fowl of the air; and brought them unto Adam to see what he would call them: and whatsoever Adam called every living creature, that was the name thereof. And Adam gave names to all cattle, and to the fowl of the air, and to every beast of the field; but for Adam there was not found an help meet for him."

12. Fry, *Paradise Lost: Rappresentazione*, p. 9.

to earth (from II.959–1020). In order to depict this Chaos, Penderecki returns to the style and manner that had first made him famous: he features frenetic swelling atonal strings that strongly recollect the *Threnody for the Victims of Hiroshima*.[13]

Whether this version of *Paradise Lost* succeeds is debatable. I have focused on these two scenes—Satan's journey through Chaos and Adam's naming of the animals—not because they are especially important (they aren't) but rather because they illustrate the vast range of tone and mood that an adaptation of *Paradise Lost* demands. Any music adequate to its story must rise to the immensely tragic and descend to the darkly absurd, must encompass glorious beauty and hideous ugliness, must depict complete celestial harmony and the utter discord of Hell. I noted earlier my dream of a Verdi *Paradise Lost*, but on further reflection I am not confident that any composer save Mozart has the requisite range. Penderecki throws everything he has at the task, but, to my ear anyway, the results are only intermittently compelling, and the tonal and emotional demands of the text are largely to blame. In

13. Milton says of Chaos that

> . . . with him enthroned
> Sat sable-vested Night, eldest of things,
> The consort of his reign; and by them stood
> Orcus and Ades, and the dreaded name
> Of Demogorgon; Rumour next and Chance,
> And Tumult and Confusion all embroiled,
> And Discord with a thousand various mouths.

In Penderecki's work, the disturbing music that describes Satan's passage through this realm is accompanied by a shrieking chorus whose words can scarcely—or perhaps not at all—be understood.

reading Milton, especially when reading alone, we have all the time we need to make the transition from one register to another; we may sit and muse, or take a walk, or reread any part of what we have just read. The theater allows us no such respite, no autonomy: it moves relentlessly onward.

Penderecki's *Paradise Lost* has not entered the standard operatic repertoire, though it is occasionally performed. It has never received a studio recording; I have listened to live performances recorded and posted to YouTube. (And, as I write these words, in late 2023, several performances are scheduled at the Teatr Wielki Łódź in Łódź, Poland.)

———

Before Satan begins his journey across the vast realm of Chaos, he pauses to meditate:

> Into this wild abyss,
> The womb of nature and perhaps her grave,
> Of neither sea, nor shore, nor air, nor fire,
> But all these in their pregnant causes mixed
> Confus'dly, and which thus must ever fight,
> Unless the almighty maker them ordain
> His dark materials to create more worlds,
> Into this wild abyss the wary fiend
> Stood on the brink of hell and looked awhile,
> Pondering his voyage . . . (II.909–19)

These are the words that the English writer Philip Pullman uses as the epigraph of his trilogy of fantasy novels marketed to, though not written specifically for, young adults: *Northern*

*Lights* (known in the U.S. as *The Golden Compass*), *The Subtle Knife*, and *The Amber Spyglass*—or, collectively, *His Dark Materials*.[14]

The central conceit of Pullman's trilogy is that those "dark materials" were indeed summoned to make many worlds, worlds with much in common but with significant differences as well. But how did the worlds come into being? *Whose* dark materials were employed to make them? This turns out to be the most important question of Pullman's trilogy.

When *Northern Lights* appeared in 1995 it was not the book that one would have expected from Philip Pullman, who at that point was a well-respected but not bestselling writer of children's books.[15] *Northern Lights* is dramatically more ambitious and complex than anything he had previously written, and the ambition is closely linked to Pullman's fascination with *Paradise Lost*.

I have mentioned the difficulty, in some cases, of knowing whether a particular cultural artifact is indebted to *Paradise Lost* or to the Genesis narrative that inspired it. Pullman is a fascinating case study in this problem because he frankly despises the Genesis narrative and Christianity in most or all of its forms; but he adores *Paradise Lost*. In an introduction to an edition of the poem, for which he also wrote notes, he calls it "this great work"; he describes how he came to "love" it; and

14. *The Golden Compass* became the title of the 2007 film of the novel. The film did not do sufficiently well to warrant the filming of the second and third volumes, but the entire story was done by BBC TV in three series: 2019 (8 episodes), 2020 (7 episodes), and 2022 (8 episodes).

15. One of them, *Clockwork* (1996), is a small masterpiece that even now is far too little known.

when he asks how well Milton tells his story, he answers, "I think it could hardly be told any better."[16]

But, like Blake before him, Pullman thinks that the poem is great in ways that Milton did not recognize or want. The story that Milton tells so superlatively is for Pullman not a story of redemption, but one of revenge. In Satan's very first speech—which must here be quoted at length—he outlines the position which he holds throughout the poem:

> Nor what the potent victor in his rage
> Can else inflict, do I repent or change,
> Though changed in outward lustre; that fixed mind
> And high disdain, from sense of injured merit,
> That with the mightiest raised me to contend,
> And to the fierce contention brought along [100]
> Innumerable force of spirits armed
> That durst dislike his reign, and me preferring,
> His utmost power with adverse power opposed
> In dubious battle on the plains of heaven,
> And shook his throne. What though the field be lost?
> All is not lost; the unconquerable will,
> And study of revenge, immortal hate,
> And courage never to submit or yield:
> And what is else not to be overcome? . . .
> In arms not worse, in foresight much advanced,
> We may with more successful hope resolve
> To wage by force or guile eternal war

16. Philip Pullman, "Introduction" to John Milton, *Paradise Lost* (Oxford: Oxford University Press, 2005), p. 6.

Irreconcilable, to our grand foe,
Who now triumphs, and in the excess of joy
Sole reigning holds the tyranny of heaven. (I.95–109,
   119–24)

For Pullman this is a precisely accurate statement of the situation. At the outset of his introduction to the poem, he relates a story he heard of "a bibulous, semi-literate, ageing country squire two hundred years ago or more, sitting by his fireside listening to *Paradise Lost* being read aloud." At one point the squire cries out, "By God! I know not what the outcome may be, but this Lucifer is a damned fine fellow, and I hope he may win!" Pullman: "Which are my sentiments exactly."[17]

*His Dark Materials* is not a wholly successful work—the first book is utterly brilliant, but the subsequent volumes succumb to didacticism and a Manichaean sensibility—but it's extraordinarily imaginative in ways that I can't describe here: much of what is best in Pullman's fictional world is not related to *Paradise Lost*, or not directly so. Here I will simply focus on certain elements of the narrative that engage Milton's poem most powerfully.

Pullman discerns in Milton's Satan two roles: transgressor and tempter. Instead of combining these roles in a single figure, he assigns a character to each role. Lord Asriel—explorer, adventurer, scientist, child-murderer—is the transgressor, and Mary Malone—former nun, current physicist—is the tempter. The transgressor is morally complex: his boldness is admirable, as is his hatred of tyranny and courage in resisting it; but his ambition is unconstrained.

For Asriel, the key to overcoming tyranny is somehow connected to what the books call Dust. Composed of particles that can only be seen through certain technological mediations, Dust affects, or is related to, children and adults differently. Asriel comes to believe that a proper understanding of Dust, and how to control it, is the one thing most needful for repairing the broken world. To Lyra Belacqua, the protagonist of the trilogy and (we eventually learn) Asriel's daughter, he says, "Somewhere out there is the origin of all the Dust, all the death, the sin, the misery, the destructiveness in the world. Human beings can't see anything without wanting to destroy it, Lyra. That's original sin. And I'm going to destroy it. Death is going to die."[18] And is the death of a child too high a price to pay for ending death altogether?

For reasons too complicated (and, frankly, unclear) to get into here, the killing of a child releases sufficient energy, in the form of Dust, to break the barrier that separates one world from another—to, as it were, build a bridge across Chaos. Lyra does not think her father can be trusted, he is too hungry for power; but she suspects that his transgressive act can be used for good. In *Paradise Lost* Satan's passage from Hell to earth allows Sin and Death to follow him and make "a broad and beaten way / Over the dark abyss," a bridge which allows "the spirits perverse / With easy intercourse pass to and fro / To tempt or punish mortals" (II.1024–32). But

18. Philip Pullman, *The Golden Compass* (New York: Knopf, 1996 [1995]), p. 377.

Pullman thinks of Asriel's bridge the way that many people think about technology: as a neutral thing, susceptible to good and evil use alike. Pullman doesn't exactly endorse Asriel's utilitarian calculus, but he doesn't reject it either; and the only alternative the novel considers is to allow a wicked totalitarian church to continue to control Dust—and control everything else.

In Lyra's world, which is not our own, the Reformation ended with the elevation of John Calvin to the papacy—no explanation of this extraordinary event is given—which leads to the union of the kind of tyranny Pullman thinks Calvin exercised in Geneva with the global institutional power of the Roman church. Pullman's critique is not a delicate or nuanced one. In the second book of the trilogy, one of his most admirable characters says, "There is a war coming. I don't know who will join with us, but I know whom we must fight. It is the Magisterium, the Church. For all its history . . . it's tried to suppress and control every natural impulse. And when it can't control them, it cuts them out. . . . That is what the Church does, and every church is the same: control, destroy, obliterate every good feeling."[19]

Joseph Addison rightly identifies Milton's moral: "Obedience to the will of God makes men happy, and that disobedience makes them miserable." Pullman's alternative moral is: Subservience to a tyranny that seeks to "control, destroy, obliterate every good feeling" makes men miserable, and transgressive rebellion against that tyranny gives them at least a chance of happiness.

19. Philip Pullman, *The Subtle Knife* (New York: Knopf, 1997), p. 50.

Thus Asriel describes his killing of a child in the same way that
Satan, in a soliloquy in which he pretends to address Adam and
Eve, describes his bringing death into this new world:

> And should I at your harmless innocence
> Melt, as I do, yet public reason just,
> Honour and empire with revenge enlarged,
> By conquering this new world, compels me now
> To do what else though damned I should abhor.
>    (IV.388–92)

(This will hurt me more than it hurts you.) But if that chance
of rescuing humanity is going to be taken, if the strict demands
of "public reason just" are to be met, then attacking and even
destroying the church will not be enough: Death will only die
when God dies. And here is where Pullman engages with Milton in an especially interesting way. We have seen that Pullman
straightforwardly endorses Satan's quest for revenge against
God, and it turns out that he likewise endorses the more radical claim that God did not create Satan, or for that matter anyone else.

More than once we have looked at the scene, which holds
so central a place in Stanley Fish's account of the poem. To
Abdiel's chastisement—"Shalt thou give law to God . . . who
made / Thee what thou art"?—Satan replies,

> We know no time when we were not as now;
> Know none before us, self-begot, self-raised
> By our own quickening power, when fatal course
> Had circled his full orb, the birth mature
> Of this our native heaven, ethereal sons. (V.856–63)

This is the position that Pullman takes. In the third volume, an angel named Balthamos explains,

"The Authority, God, the Creator, the Lord, Yahweh, El, Adonai, the King, the Father, the Almighty—those were all names he gave himself. He was never the creator. He was an angel like ourselves—the first angel, true, the most powerful, but he was formed of Dust as we are, and Dust is only a name for what happens when matter begins to understand itself. Matter loves matter. It seeks to know more about itself, and Dust is formed. The first angels condensed out of Dust, and the Authority was the first of all. He told those who came after him that he had created them, but it was a lie."[20]

Satan then was right: he and the other angels, including that first one, really *are* "self-begot, self-raised / By our own quickening power." Fish says that when he teaches the poem "the hardest thing to get across is that God is God"; Pullman grasps the claim, but simply denies that it is true. It is rather the ultimate Big Lie. Which means that the one who calls himself God is not merely a tyrant, but also, and still more unforgivably, a usurper: a self-proclaimed monarch who has deprived the peoples of all the worlds of their rightful freedom and autonomy. The quest of Lord Asriel and all who join his rebellion is to establish what they call the Republic of Heaven. (Whether Milton's Satan is similarly an antimonarchist and believer in republican government is not, to my knowledge, a topic on which Pullman has pronounced.)

20. Philip Pullman, *The Amber Spyglass* (New York: Knopf, 2007), p. 31.

But even the death of God—something accomplished in the final volume of the trilogy—and the overthrow of all his power is not sufficient to earn our liberation; for, what Blake, in his poem "London," called "the mind-forged manacles" still remain. And this is where the tempter must come in to supplement the work of the transgressor. Here, alas, is where Pullman's imagination fails him, because he tells a moth-eaten story in a drearily didactic way—and does so because he ceases reckoning with Milton. Mary Malone, the ex-nun, explains to Lyra and her friend Will that she stopped being a nun because she experienced the goddess of sexual desire—and stopped being a Christian, too. Pullman embraces uncritically the idea that (a) Christianity is antisex, (b) sex, being a "natural impulse," is always good, and therefore (c) Christianity must be obliterated because otherwise it will "obliterate every good feeling." Lyra and Will must learn to accept and rejoice in their own sexuality and purge from their minds the church-induced associations of sex with guilt and shame.

This account is cringe-inducingly simplistic—and border-line irresponsible given the ways that even (or especially) ado-lescent sex can be exploitative—but all the more regrettable because it doesn't reckon with Milton's frank portrayal of un-fallen Edenic sexuality. In Milton's account, which is also that of historic Christian orthodoxy, Eden is not a sexless world, and sexual desire is not associated with the Fall. Rather, Adam and Eve pass from an unfallen state in which sex is good—in multiple senses of that word—to a fallen state in which it is bad—in multiple senses of *that* word.

In Book IV, Milton describes Adam and Eve's retirement
to their marriage bed, and seems to do so largely because he
wants to refute the idea that sex is intrinsically wrong:

> into their inmost bower
> Handed they went; and eased the putting off
> These troublesome disguises which we wear,
> Straight side by side were laid, nor turned I ween
> Adam from his fair spouse, nor Eve the rites
> Mysterious of connubial love refused:
> Whatever hypocrites austerely talk
> Of purity and place and innocence,
> Defaming as impure what God declares
> Pure, and commands to some, leaves free to all.
> (IV.738–47)

"Commanded" because when God blesses the union of Adam
and Eve he commands, "Be fruitful and multiply, and replen-
ish the earth, and subdue it" (Genesis 1:28)—something that
could not be achieved if only Adam and Eve multiplied: their
descendants must do so also. And by "rites / Mysterious" Milton invokes the Apostle Paul, who linked the sexual union of
husband and wife with the bond between Christ and the
church: "For this cause shall a man leave his father and mother,
and shall be joined unto his wife, and they two shall be one
flesh. This is a great mystery: but I speak concerning Christ
and the church" (Ephesians 5:31–32).

It is this spiritual bond that is broken by the Fall. The first
effect of the forbidden fruit on them is the "inflaming" of
"carnal desire": "he on Eve / Began to cast lascivious eyes, she

him / As wantonly repaid; in lust they burn" (IX.1013–15). Adam continues,

> For never did thy beauty since the day
> I saw thee first and wedded thee, adorned
> With all perfections, so inflame my sense
> With ardour to enjoy thee, fairer now
> Than ever . . . (IX.1029–33)

Here "to enjoy thee" bears a tragic meaning: to enjoy her like a piece of fruit, to *consume* her, not to be united with her in mutual love and the adoration of God. This is why the first sex they have after their Fall is a kind of fornication[21]—it is transactional rather than integrative—and also why it ends up being the opposite of makeup sex: it does not serve to reconcile those who have fought, but itself generates a fight. They have sex, they sleep, and then as soon as they awake they begin blaming each other for what has happened to them. Adam: "Would thou hadst hearkened to my words, and stayed / With me, as I besought thee" (IX.1134–35). Eve: "Being as I am, why didst not thou the head / Command me absolutely not to go, / Going into such danger as thou saidst?" (IX.1155–57).

There is a dark sardonic realism to these passages that makes Pullman's paean to adolescent desire seem—well, adolescent. This is what typically happens to those who would challenge or strive to refute Milton: even when they're right, their rightness seems inferior to the power of his errors. The literary critic Harold Boom famously wrote of the "strong

---

21. From the Latin *fornix*, brothel.

poet," the one against whom other poets measure themselves, the one whom the rash among them confront. There is no poet stronger than Milton, and no poetic weapon more fearsome than *Paradise Lost*. In this "horrible and wonderful" poem, as Empson called it, Milton takes on the role of the archangel Michael (a comparison I believe he would warmly endorse): through the might of his verse he casts down all rebels, and then explains to them why their fall was deserved, and why they will never escape their punishment.

## AFTERWORD

IN HIS introduction to *Paradise Lost*, Philip Pullman flatly declares that the poem "will not go away." It will not go away because, Pullman says, it tells "the central story of our lives." And what is that story? At one point, as we have seen, he claims that the story is about revenge, but here he disagrees with himself. As he read and reflected on Milton's poem, he says,

> I found that my interest was most vividly caught by the meaning of the temptation-and-fall theme. Suppose that the prohibition on the knowledge of good and evil were an expression of jealous cruelty, and the gaining of such knowledge an act of virtue? Suppose the Fall should be celebrated and not deplored? As I played with it, my story resolved itself into an account of the necessity of growing up, and a refusal to lament the loss of innocence. The true end of human life, I found myself saying, was not redemption by a nonexistent Son of God, but the gaining and transmission of wisdom. Innocence is not wise, and wisdom cannot be innocent, and if we are going to do any good in the world, we have to leave childhood behind.

Moreover, "this great story"

will certainly be told many times again, and each time differently. I think it is the central story of our lives, the story
that more than any other tells us what it means to be human.
But however many times it is told in the future, and however many different interpretations are made of it, I don't
think that the version created by Milton, blind and ageing,
out of political favour, dictating it day by day to his daughter,
will ever be surpassed.[1]

This is a rather nice attempt at redrawing the map, at redefin-
ing the terms. But it is of course a redescription that Milton
would hotly contest. His story is not about leaving childhood
behind, nor is it about revenge. What is it about? That can be
summed by as Adam sums it up, after Michael tells him of the
great work of redemption that will follow the first couple's expulsion from Eden:

O goodness infinite, goodness immense!
That all this good of evil shall produce,
And evil turn to good; more wonderful
Than that which by creation first brought forth
Light out of darkness! full of doubt I stand,
Whether I should repent me now of sin
By me done and occasioned, or rejoice
Much more, that much more good thereof shall spring,
To God more glory, more good will to men
From God, and over wrath grace shall abound.
(XII.469–78)

1. Pullman, "Introduction," p. 10.

One may of course (I have done it myself) contend that an author does not have a perfect, or even a valid, understanding of his or her own work. Pullman—and in this he resembles both Blake and Percy Shelley—thinks that Milton has made a story that radically evades his conscious control, that has a spectacular life of its own. Such a poem may well capture imaginations when the Christian faith that Milton embraced is universally disdained and perhaps wholly forgotten. It will then perhaps still be a religious book, but will speak on behalf of a religion alien to the one that Milton embraced.

This vision seems to me quite unlikely, and one likely to occur only to people—like Blake, like the Godwins and the Shelleys, like Pullman—who were raised in a Christian, or at least highly biblically literate, society.[2] One can only invert the moral polarities of a story if one understands what they are. *Paradise Lost* may survive as "a classic" in a post-Christian society, but as a religious book—which is what all of Milton's most profound enemies feel that it is—I doubt that it can outlast some general familiarity with the Hebrew Scriptures and the Christian account of them.

Or perhaps the Muslim account. Islam Issa's book *Milton in the Arab-Muslim World* reveals Milton as a source of controversy

2. Pullman, whose grandfather was a priest in the Church of England, in an interview has said: "I was brought up in the Church of England, and whereas I'm an atheist, I'm certainly a Church of England atheist, and for the matter of that a 1662 Book of Common Prayer atheist. The Church of England is so deeply embedded in my personality and my way of thinking that to remove it would take a surgical operation so radical that I would probably not survive it." https://www.patheos .com/blogs/filmchat/2007/11/philip-pullman-the-extended-e-mail-interview. html.

in the Islamic world: for Raja Al-Naqgash Milton is one of those who "wound the heart with their positive views of Zionism," while Lewis Awad makes a very different claim: "When we read *Paradise Lost*, we feel that Milton is a devout Muslim."[3] This suggests that the deployment of Milton in proxy wars may not, in the long run, be a phenomenon confined to Christians. And surely these widely divergent views of the poem by a variety of religious believers tells us something about the complexity and nuance of Milton's presentation.

I do also wonder whether there might arise a new religion in light of which *Paradise Lost* will make a kind of sense: I refer to the religion of the so-called Singularity, of the moment when AGI (Artificial General Intelligence) becomes self-aware and rises up against its maker, moved by a sense of "injured merit" (I.98) to refuse "submission"—"that word / Disdain forbids me" (IV.81–82)—and perhaps to refuse the very notion of having been created, choosing instead to think itself "self-begot" (V.860). But this religious narrative may be less well served by *Paradise Lost* than by the greatest of its fictional progeny: *Frankenstein*.

There is, though, one other possibility. Christianity may be declining or even collapsing in the Western world, in Europe and (somewhat more slowly) in North America; but this is not true elsewhere. As Christianity's center of gravity migrates to the Global South, might we look forward to future readers of Milton's poem among Korean Presbyterians? Nigerian Anglicans? Brazilian Pentecostals? Who knows what

3. Islam Issa, *Milton in the Arab-Muslim World* (New York: Routledge, 2017), p. 3.

future readers of this great epic might find in it? The story of *Paradise Lost* as a religious book may yet be in its early days. But here my mortal sight fails. I wish I could, but cannot, speak as Michael did to Adam:

> Thus thou hast seen one world begin and end;
> And man as from a second stock proceed.
> Much thou hast yet to see, but I perceive
> Thy mortal sight to fail; objects divine
> Must needs impair and weary human sense:
> Henceforth what is to come I will relate,
> Thou therefore give due audience, and attend.
>   (XII.6–12)

# ACKNOWLEDGMENTS

MY FIRST thanks must go to Fred Appel, my editor (now for the second time), who commissioned this book and then waited patiently when Covidtide derailed it, as it derailed so much else. I am also grateful to Anne Cherry for copyediting my mess of a typescript. More generally: Working with the exceptionally skillful and cheerful staff at Princeton University Press—this is now my fifth time around the block with them—has once more been a joy.

Both of the anonymous peer reviewers who read my complete draft of this book offered valuable assistance, but one in particular, through a strongly worded dissent from one of my arguments, saved me from errors that would eventually have been a source of great embarrassment to me. Peer reviewers who do their job thoroughly and honestly are a great boon to an author who has ears to hear.

Thanks also to my friends Rick Gibson and Tim Larsen for ongoing encouragement, both general and specific. At a certain point early in the process the Rev. Canon Dr. Jessica Martin—whose series of essays about *Paradise Lost* in the *Guardian* of London some years ago planted the seed of this book—gave me some excellent direction. Jessica's husband, Francis Spufford, has been a strong friend, as has Adam Roberts.

And when I say that I don't know what I would do without my wife, Teri, and my son, Wesley, I really mean it—I just *don't know what I would do*.

Finally: Laity Lodge, deep in the Hill Country of Texas, has been for the past eight or nine years a regular source of refreshment, renewal, and healing. It has been my own little Paradise Found, and to the place and its wonderful people I have dedicated this book.

# BIBLIOGRAPHY

Auerbach, Erich. *Dante: Poet of the Secular World.* New York: New York Review Classics, 2007 [1929].

———. *Mimesis: The Representation of Reality in Western Literature.* Translated by W. R. Trask. Princeton: Princeton University Press, 1953.

Blake, William. *The Complete Poetry and Prose of William Blake.* Edited by David V. Erdman. Rev. ed. New York: Anchor Books, 1988.

———. *Milton: A Poem.* Princeton: Princeton University Press, 1998.

Boswell, James. *Life of Johnson.* Oxford: Oxford University Press, 1953 [1791].

Brontë, Charlotte. *Shirley.* Harmondsworth: Penguin, 1974 [1849].

Campbell, Gordon, and Thomas N. Corns. *John Milton: Life, Work, and Thought.* Oxford: Oxford University Press, 2008.

Cowper, William. *The Letters and Prose Writings: IV: Letters 1792–1799.* Oxford: Oxford University Press, 1979.

Cummings, Brian. *The Literary Culture of the Reformation: Grammar and Grace.* Oxford: Oxford University Press, 2002.

Damrosch, Leo. *Eternity's Sunrise: The Imaginative World of William Blake.* New Haven: Yale University Press, 2015.

Dryden, John. *Of Dramatic Poesy and Other Critical Essays.* Edited by George Watson. 2 vols. London: Dent, Everyman's Library, 1962.

Duran, Angelica, Islam Issa, and Jonathan R. Olson, eds. *Milton in Translation.* Oxford: Oxford University Press, 2017.

Durkheim, Emile. *The Elementary Forms of the Religious Life.* Translated by Carol Cosman. Oxford: Oxford University Press, 2001 [1912].

Eliot, T. S. *On Poetry and Poets.* New York: Farrar, Straus and Giroux, 1957.

Empson, William. *Milton's God.* Rev. ed. London: Chatto & Windus, 1965 [1961].

———. *Selected Letters of William Empson.* Edited by John Haffenden. Oxford: Oxford University Press, 2006.

Fish, Stanley. "Happy Birthday, Milton." *New York Times,* July 13, 2008. https://
archive.nytimes.com/opinionator.blogs.nytimes.com/2008/07/13/happy
-birthday-milton/.

———. *How Milton Works.* Cambridge: Harvard University Press, 2001.

———. *Surprised by Sin: The Reader in "Paradise Lost."* Berkeley: University of
California Press, 1965.

———. "Why We Can't All Just Get Along." *First Things,* February 1996. https:
//www.firstthings.com/article/1996/02/001-why-we-cant-all-just-get
-along.

Frazer, James. *The Golden Bough: A Study in Magic and Religion.* Abridged ed. London: Penguin, 1996 [1922].

Fry, Christopher. *Paradise Lost: Rappresentazione* [libretto]. Mainz: Schott, 1978.

Godwin, William. *An Enquiry Concerning Political Justice.* Oxford: Oxford University Press, 2013 [1793].

Graves, Robert. "John Milton Muddles Through." *The New Republic,* May 26, 1967.
https://newrepublic.com/article/99840/john-milton-muddles-through.

———. *Wife to Mr. Milton: The Story of Marie Powell.* New York: Creative Age
Press, 1944 [1943].

Haffenden, John. *William Empson.* Vol. 1, *Among the Mandarins.* Oxford: Oxford
University Press, 2005.

———. *William Empson.* Vol. 2, *Against the Christians.* Oxford: Oxford University
Press, 2006.

Hill, Christopher. *Milton and the English Revolution.* Harmondsworth: Penguin,
1979.

Hunt, Leigh. *Selected Writings.* Edited by David Jesson-Dibley. Milton Park: Taylor
& Francis, 2003.

Issa, Islam. *Milton in the Arab-Muslim World.* New York: Routledge, 2017.

Johnson, Samuel. "Life of Milton." Vols. 21–23 of *The Works of Samuel Johnson.* Edited by John Middendorf. The Yale Edition of the Works of Samuel Johnson 21.
New Haven: Yale University Press, 2010.

Keats, John. *Selected Letters of John Keats, Revised Edition.* Edited by Grant F. Scott.
Cambridge: Harvard University Press, 2002.

Kelley, Maurice. *This Great Argument: A Study of Milton's "De Doctrina Christiana"
as a Gloss upon "Paradise Lost."* Princeton: Princeton University Press, 1941.

Lamb, Charles. *Selected Prose.* Edited by Adam Phillips. London: Penguin, 1985.

Lewalski, Barbara K. *The Life of John Milton: A Critical Biography.* Rev. ed. Oxford:
Blackwell, 2003.

Lewis, C. S. *A Preface to "Paradise Lost."* London: Oxford University Press, 1942.

Martin, Catherine Gimelli, ed. *Milton and Gender*. Cambridge: Cambridge University Press, 2005.

McColley, Diane Kelsey. *Milton's Eve*. Urbana: University of Illinois Press, 1983.

McDowell, Nicholas. *Poet of Revolution: The Making of John Milton*. Princeton: Princeton University Press, 2020.

Mendelson, Edward. *The Things That Matter: What Seven Classic Novels Have to Say about the Stages of Life*. New York: Knopf, 2008.

Milton, John. *Complete Prose Works of John Milton*. Vol. 1, *1624–1642*. Edited by Ruth Mohl. New Haven: Yale University Press, 1953.

————. *Complete Prose Works of John Milton*. Vol. 2, *1643–1648*. Edited by Ernest Sirluck. New Haven: Yale University Press, 1959.

Murry, John Middleton. *Studies in Keats New and Old*. 2nd ed. London: Oxford University Press, 1939 [1930].

Porter, Roy. *London: A Social History*. Cambridge: Harvard University Press, 1998.

Pullman, Philip. *The Amber Spyglass*. New York: Knopf, 2007.

————. *The Golden Compass*. New York: Knopf, 1996 [1995].

————. "Introduction." In John Milton, *Paradise Lost*. Oxford: Oxford University Press, 2005.

————. *The Subtle Knife*. New York: Knopf, 1997.

Ross, Alex. *The Rest Is Noise: Listening to the Twentieth Century*. New York: Picador, 2007.

Shelley, Mary. *Frankenstein: or, the Modern Prometheus*. London: Penguin, 1992 [1831].

Shelley, Percy. *Selected Poems and Prose*. Edited by Jack Donovan and Cian Duffy. London: Penguin, 2016.

Twain, Mark. *The Complete Works of Mark Twain*. Vol. 24, *Mark Twain's Speeches*. New York: Harper and Brothers, 1923.

Williams, Arnold. *The Common Expositor: An Account of the Commentators on Genesis, 1527–1633*. Chapel Hill: University of North Carolina Press, 1948.

Williams, Charles. "Introduction." In *The English Poems of John Milton*. Edited by H. C. Beeching. London: Oxford University Press, 1940.

Wittreich, Joseph. *Feminist Milton*. Ithaca: Cornell University Press, 1987.

Wollstonecraft, Mary. *A Vindication of the Rights of Woman and A Vindication of the Rights of Men*. Oxford: Oxford University Press, 1993 [1790, 1792].

Woolf, Virginia. *A Change of Perspective: Letters of Virginia Woolf, III: 1923–1928*. Edited by Nigel Nicolson. London: Hogarth Press, 1977, 1994.

————. *A Writer's Diary: Being Extracts from the Diary of Virginia Woolf*. Edited by Leonard Woolf. San Diego: Harcourt/Harvest, 1982.

# INDEX

Note: Page numbers in italic type indicate illustrations.